Volume
1

BRIGID BISHOP

Uncloaking the Tarot

Uncloaking the Tarot

©2001 Brigid Bishop
TXu001015838 / 2001-10-01,
First Revision 2011
Freeland, PA 18224 USA
www.brigidbishop.com

A Note of Thanks

Friends Along the Way

special thank you to my friend from Elk Grove, Illinois, Helen Robles, who has been an ever present and patient comrade since I first produced this book back in 2001.

I would also like to thank my friend, Lisa Raymoure-Cooper, in Hudson, Wisconsin, for her continuous support and encouragement as I revised this work a decade later.

Dedication

This book is dedicated to the thousands of clients who have contacted me over the last ten years seeking guidance through the Tarot. I hope that, in conducting our sessions, I have helped you along on your journey as all of you have assisted me. Thank you!

Brigid Bishop

Other Books by Brigid Bishop

Uncloaking the Tarot, Workbook and Tarot Journal, November 2011

Brigid Bishop's Little Book of Magick Spells, November 2011

The Dating Game: Insights into Affairs of The Heart, April 2010

Table of Contents

Chapter

Background and Overview

Uncloaking the Tarot

Welcome to "***Uncloaking the Tarot***". I hope that by reading and digesting the information presented herein, you will gain a comprehensive understanding and appreciation of the Tarot, and have the ability to pass this knowledge along to your friends and family.

The lesson plan presented within this text is meant to remove the myth and mystery surrounding the Tarot, and to be presented in such a manner as to educate the general public, heretofore not presented with sufficient information to make an intelligent judgment on the use of the Tarot as a personal growth mechanism.

The Tarot dates back to Ancient Egypt and has changed and evolved through the centuries. There are many different decks that have been adapted by many different cultures.

For the purpose of this educational manuscript, we will use the Universal Waite Deck, as this learning tool is for the beginner and intermediate student of the Tarot and this deck contains the most universally recognized symbolism of the Tarot Deck. Future writings will encompass the cultural adaptations of the deck, but for the novice, we shall stay with that which is considered to be a "***standard***".

What the Tarot Is, What the Tarot is Not

What the Tarot is, is a tool for stimulating personal spiritual growth. The Tarot, known by the general public as primarily a divinatory tool, has much more productive uses than divination for the enlightened and educated individual.

What the Tarot is not, is a fortune telling mechanism that will predict exactly what the course of events of your life will be. Although the Tarot can be used effectively for divination, the Tarot will only present to the Reader what will happen if the current course of events remains unaltered, so Free Will always allows you to alter the future presented in the cards, either in a positive or adverse manner. It is key for the Reader and the Querent to mark specifically what path they are on consciously in order for a Reading to be an effective consultation of the esoteric.

Myths and Misconceptions

Myths and misconceptions concerning the Tarot abound. One popular myth is that you should never read your own cards. Let me dispel that for you right now with one logical statement: The Tarot is meant to be a meditational tool, assisting us with the introspection process, if we are not to read our own cards, then how will they be an effective tool for our own personal spiritual growth?

Although there is danger that we will project our hopes and fears onto the spread when we read our own cards, this can be avoided if prior to reading we focus on our question and meditate on the statement "not my hopes, not my fears, but the truth". Maintaining this meditational sentence in our consciousness while working with the cards will assist us in eliminating any corruption of a personal self-reading.

Another misconception is that the Tarot has something to do with the practice of some dark, magickal, or evil force. Call it what you will. Quite to the contrary, the Tarot is a holy and mystical part of understanding what our souls were meant to do on this earthly plane, what lessons we were put here to learn, and how to better serve the human race. Understanding with others begins with understanding ourselves. How can we interact effectively with the rest of the human race if we lack the basic understanding of the psychological and emotional motives that drive us to behave in the manners that we do. The Tree of Life, as presented by the Holy Qabalah, is an ancient and spiritual path to wholeness of the soul, there is nothing evil about it. The Tarot brings us closer to the God and Goddess within, and helps us to live among the various states of evolution our sisters and brothers on this earthly plane exist in, in peace and harmony.

The Tarot Deck

The Tarot Deck consists of 78 cards. 22 of these cards are referred to as the "Major Arcana" and the remaining 56 are known as the "Minor Arcana".

The *Major Arcana* are the most powerful cards in the deck. The twenty-two archetypical members represent archetypes of the human soul's journey through development. Each member has powerful spiritual and divinatory implications; we will review each card individually, in order to expedite a comprehensive understanding of the deck.

The Major Arcana are drenched in symbolism and relate to not only reincarnation, internal development, external forces, numerology and astrology, but tie in to nearly every esoteric principle that exists.

When a member of the Major Arcana appears in a spread, it represents forces that are beyond the Querent's control. They tend to represent either the actions of others who have influence over the situation, or the role of fate, karma, destiny, or whatever you prefer to refer to it as.

The important thing to remember when working with the cards is that we must learn to accept the things that are beyond our control, and focus on those things which we can control (ourselves). Remember this: Never let something that is out of your control upset you, the only factor we can control in this life is ourselves. If we come to a challenging situation in life, reflect upon what factors you could and could not control, and adjust your behaviors accordingly. With this in mind, the Tarot can help you look inward for guidance.

The *Minor Arcana* consists of "court" cards and the "pip" cards in four suits. The court cards are the Page, Knight, Queen, and King, the pip cards consist of the ace through ten. If you noticed that this almost sounds like the structure of a modern deck of playing cards, you are on track with the course of study already. The modern deck arose from the Tarot, the Page has been eliminated, and the balance of the deck remains intact. The Knight is commonly referred to as the Jack, and the four suits of the Tarot are commonly called: Wands, Cups, Swords, and Pentacles, replaced respectively with Clubs, Hearts, Spades, and Diamonds.

Tarot Decks sometimes vary the names of the suits, common alternate names are as follows; Pentacles, also referred to as "Coins", "Shields" or "Disks". Wands are sometimes called "Rods", "Staffs" or "Spears". Cups may sometimes be referred to as "Hearts", "Horns" or "Waterskins". Swords in some decks are referred to as "Daggers". The decks of different cultures may have various alternate suit names, but the meanings remain the same, regardless of what we refer to the suit as.

The Suit of Wands refers to action being taken. It is associated with the Element of Fire, the South Quarter of the Circle, the Season of Spring, and the time of day of Noon. Typically, a Wand appearing in a spread will indicate movement or action of some kind. The Qabalah assigns the Letter I from the ancient Hebraic Alphabet to it. Astrologically, the signs of Aries, Leo and Sagittarius are represented by the Wands.

The Suit of Cups is associated with emotion, love and human relationships, when predominant in a spread it nearly always pertains to matters of the heart. The Season of Summer, the West

Quarter of the Circle, the Element of Water, the Letter O and Dusk are associated with Cups. The corresponding Astrological signs are Pisces, Cancer and Scorpio.

The Swords are representative of the Autumn, of things perhaps coming to an end. Many of the pip cards in the Swords Suit are associated with pain, or painful forced change, but not all. Swords represent the East Quarter of the Circle, the Element of Air, the Letter E, and Dawn. Swords represent the intellectual in many cases. The Astrological signs of Aquarius, Gemini and Libra are reflected in this Suit.

The fourth Suit, Pentacles, represents all that is material, and successes on the earthly plane. Work and family are closely associated with this Suit which is associated with Winter, the Element of Earth, the Letter A, the North Quarter of the Circle, and Night. The Astrological signs that correspond are Taurus, Virgo and Capricorn.

Are you beginning to see how Tarot ties into all that is esoteric? If not, by the end of this manuscript, you will.

The Care and Handling of the Tarot

While many believe that the Tarot should be wrapped in a black cloth and cleansed with sea salt or another symbolic "clean" substance, i.e. holy water, oil, sunlight, the light of the full moon, I find that "bonding" with your cards is most effective in ensuring your working well with your deck.

By bonding, I mean that you should connect with your cards spiritually, on an individual basis. So if holy water is symbolic to you of purity, by all means, use this to clear any negative vibrations from your cards, or if sea salt symbolizes cleansing, use it, but choose something that to you symbolizes purity. Your deck, especially your first deck, is a spiritual tool. Treat it as such.

The cards should be treated with respect, many wrap their cards in a black cloth, black being a neutral color that does not absorb but reflects negativity. Other cartomancers prefer to wrap their cards in white, universally recognized as the color of purity. Still others use small pouches or scarves, anything you are comfortable with will do, but be sure that you handle the cards and store them in a manner which reflects respect for their status as a spiritual tool, likened to a set of rosary beads or a crucifix.

By treating the cards with respect, you will begin to recognize the spirituality within the images. The cards have absolutely no power as inanimate objects; however, if you form a physical and psychological bond with them you will empower them when you commence reading for yourself or for others.

How to Use This Text

While utilizing this text to learn to read the tarot, keep in mind that your interpretation of the cards will be as individual as a thumbprint, many will totally bypass this introductory chapter and will have jumped right into throwing the cards and looking up the meanings, that is fine, however, if you truly wish to connect with and be adept at interpreting the Tarot, I strongly suggest that you go through the cards one by one.

If you have purchased _Uncloaking the Tarot, Workbook Companion and Tarot Journal_, along with this text, comprehensive instructions are found there. If you are working with the textbook alone I suggest you use the Universal Waite Tarot Deck, produced by U.S. Games Systems, Inc. to get the most from this text.

Begin with the card entitled The Fool. Examine the picture and use your existing knowledge of psychology, symbolism, astrology and your intuition, (your general impressions), to interpret what the card is trying to communicate to you. Make notes of your impressions if you are not using the workbook. Continue through the deck card by card, referring to the text and comparing your impressions to the interpretations provided herein. You will be pleasantly surprised at how close your interpretations of the cards are to the descriptions given here if you relax and take your time while studying the deck card by card.

Welcome to _Uncloaking the Tarot!_

The Journey Begins

Uncloaking the Tarot: The Major Arcana

The Journey Begins With The Fool

The Fool, the Number Zero, the beginning (and the end). Look at the picture on this card, how does it make you feel? A large component of Tarot Reading is individual. What thoughts or feelings does the image of The Fool provoke within you? Start a Tarot Journal and record your initial impressions of this card, over time you will be surprised at how your understanding will grow and evolve, record your novice impressions now, they will help you progress in study.

When you look at The Fool, does he not look optimistic? Carefree? Naïve? Perhaps The Fool is infantile in his emotional understanding of the world around him?

Study the picture. The Fool has his head turned upward toward the sky, indicating an innocent optimism, perhaps an enjoyment of his surroundings, yet he fails to see the cliff he is approaching. Is his white dog, the classic human companion, nipping at his heel to warn him to look where he is heading, or is he playing and enjoying his excursion with The Fool?

The background is interpreted by some as mountains that are ice-capped and cold, by others as large waves in the distance, representing the element of water. What do you see?

The sun shines brightly in the background, illuminating the entire scene and representing the element of fire.

The stick cast over The Fools' shoulder represents the Suit of Wands, also ruled by the element of fire. The stick carries all of The Fools' worldly belongings and represents the element of earth, as does the white rose he carries along with him. White is the color for purity.

The Fools' cloak contains additional symbols referring to the four elements of earth, air, fire and water, and also, if you look on the chest of The Fool you will see that his heart is imprinted on his cloak, there for all to see.

The red feather in his cap symbolizes passion (the color red) yet indicates a whimsical outlook on the world.

The Fool represents new beginnings, the absence of preconceived notions; The Fool is a blank slate waiting to be scribed upon. When The Fool appears in a spread, relative to the position he appears in, he represents a new beginning, a fresh start, openness to adventure and experience.

The Fool can also indicate foolish behaviors, selfish in nature, like a child who can only accept things on their own terms. Take note of the cavalier attitude The Fool represents, he can represent a totally self-centered adult, to know what esoteric message he is delivering to the Querent you must take the context of the entire spread into consideration, as you will see is true with all 78 cards in the deck.

The Fool represents the letter Aleph, he is ruled by the planet Uranus, which also rules the sign of Aquarius, but more important is The Fool's association with the number zero. Zero is associated with Air, for this card, the Air creates a vacuum. The vacuum can either pull knowledge and experience in, or remain in suspended animation in the self-centered hedonism of the card. If The Fool is inattentive to his path, he will meet with self-destruction, as symbolized by the card depicting him approaching the edge of a cliff. However, if The Fool is attentive, he can learn all that the elements of Fire, Water, Earth and Air (depicted by the sun, the wand, the water, and the flower in his hand on this card) have to teach him.

Consider The Fool carefully. He represents the beginning of the journey of the soul through the Tarot.

In relationship matters, The Fool represents a fresh start, a new beginning, but perhaps risking a repeat of old behaviors if a conscious effort is not made to learn from one's mistakes.

In other matters, this card will indicate a new beginning, but perhaps inattention to detail, caution the Querent to stay aware of their surroundings and seek to determine if there are hidden influences that may thwart attempts at progress.

The positive energies of this card indicate an optimistic energy; the negative tones indicate inattention and possible folly.

To divine the intentions of another when this card is prevalent, an optimistic energy will prevail in the Querent's favor.

The Magician

The Magician, able to transform and change his surroundings, (or at least appear to do so). The Number One. This card is referred to the letter Beth, and is attributed to the planet Mercury. Mercury is the ruler of both Gemini and Virgo.

The Magician is an alchemist, seeking strength, knowledge and control. The Magician holds a wand in one hand, and has a pentacle, a cup, and a sword as his tools. The Magician is learning the mystical art of alchemy and how to use the elements represented by the suits of The Tarot to change and transform his world. As The Fool becomes The Magician on his journey, he learns to use the tools of the universe to work within his environment.

On the altar before The Magician, you see a sword, a pentacle, a cup and a wand. With the wand, The Magician creates, it is a phallic symbol representing masculine fertility, with the cup he preserves himself spiritually and emotionally, with the sword, he destroys his enemies, and with the pentacle, he redeems himself. The Magician is actively invoking the powers of the elements; he possesses wisdom and is a Master of his surroundings.

He is surrounded by red flowers of passion and power, white flowers of purity, and pink flowers of love. The infinity symbol appears above his head, symbolizing his immense knowledge, the snake wrapped around his waist as a belt symbolizes wisdom and sexual temptation. The red headband on his crown indicates a passion for knowledge along with his red cloak, indicating power, and his white robe, indicating purity.

When The Magician appears in a spread, someone is controlling a situation, commanding its outcome, or manipulating events to their own benefit. Consider The Magician. What does he evoke within you? Can you feel The Magician within yourself?

The Magician may make things appear as he wishes them to be perceived. Perception is truth. What you perceive as truth may not be the same as what I may perceive, even upon having been exposed to the same set of circumstances. Be sure that you are being presented with all of the facts when dealing with The Magician; he is skilled in the art of deception.

In relationship matters, The Magician represents a need for control and a sense of insecurity or mistrust. There can well be hidden influences within the relationship, perhaps even to the point of dishonesty and infidelity.

In other matters, this card will indicate a mastery of a situation. A person will utilize all of their resources to achieve their desires.

The positive energies of this card indicate strength of will, an ability to take charge and make the most of a situation. The negative vibration of this card will indicate a person willing to achieve their goals by any means necessary, including through dishonesty and manipulation.

To divine the intentions of another when this card is prevalent, they will seek control of the situation to their own benefit.

The High Priestess

The High Priestess, symbolic of the esoteric, hidden meanings, secrets yet to be revealed, the Number Two (duality), the letter Gimel, a complex card to study.

The Priestess rests between two pillars, symbolizing balance and strength. She is wise and balanced as represented by her being situated between the two pillars which are symbolic of Boaz and Jachin as defined by the letters B and J, referencing the pillars that held up King Solomon's Temple. The colors of black and white, the eternal balancing of opposing natures, male and female, yin and yang are the essence of this card.

This card vibrates to the powers and attributes of The Moon, see the Goddess Crown she wears? It is symbolic of the waxing, full and waning cycles of the moon, also the maiden, the mother and the crone, the cycles of womanhood. Feminine energy at its purest form is expressed in the High Priestess. She is celibate as her journey here is spiritual, not physical.

Note the crescent moon rising at her feet. Cancer is ruled by The Moon, think of the secrets the depths of the ocean hold, this is the depth of the secrets The High Priestess guards. The wisdom of the ocean is the wisdom of this archetypical image, having birthed all life, the original source of the genesis of man, thus, the omni-mother of all on earth.

Emotive, yet secretive, withdrawn, perhaps hidden, cyclical, feminine, balance, physical abstinence are all energies present when she appears in a spread.

When The High Priestess appears, there are deeper hidden influences governing the situation you are inquiring about. The High Priestess is again, celibate, so physical desire and sexual activity are absent regarding the divination of this card. Her blue robes symbolize purity in love.

The High Priestess is host to hidden knowledge that at times we are not yet meant to know. She has control over the four elements of fire, earth, air and water, reflected in the cross she wears, which unlike the Christian symbol, is of equal horizontal and vertical length.

The scroll she holds is the Akasha, believed to be the record of the collective unconscious, of all that ever was or will be, and all we ever were or will be. The waters of knowledge flow at her feet and run throughout the entire deck of Tarot Cards. She indeed is a potent card, and when she appears in a spread, close attention must be paid to the cards that surround her.

When the High Priestess is active in a spread, more information exists that the Querent is not yet aware of. At times, we are not given all the information concerning a situation, as we are not yet prepared to process it. Interpret her as *"secrets yet to be revealed"*. Be aware that more knowledge will be forthcoming over time when the High Priestess is present.

In relationship matters, The High Priestess represents an absence of sexuality, it does not necessarily mean that there is a lack of desire, but love exists in a purer, higher form. This card also represents secrets being kept from each other that may take time to reveal themselves.

In other matters, this card will indicate a decision being made not through emotion, but through intellect, trying to maintain the greatest good for all involved.

The positive energies of this card indicate a purity of intention, although information may be withheld, there is no malice in failing to share all of the information available. The negative tone of this card would indicate a level of secretiveness that prevents the Querent from making a wise choice.

To divine the intentions of another when this card is prevalent, they will seek to keep that which they are hiding well concealed until they feel that the time is right to share that knowledge.

The Empress

The Empress. Think about the title. If you are a female, imagine how it would feel to be an Empress. Do you feel powerful? Do you feel duty bound to nurture those you are responsible for? Do you feel gracious and noble? Contemplate how you would feel if you, yourself, were an Empress.

The twelve stars on her brilliant crown represent the twelve signs of the zodiac, of which she has complete understanding.

The lush vegetation surrounding her represents fertility.

The heart, with the symbol of Venus upon it represents that she, too, is ruled by Venus, and that she is the Goddess of Love, the deity of femininity, sexuality, pleasure, creativity and fertility.

She is the mother and she is the wife.

She is ruled by the zodiac signs of Taurus and Libra, the sensual signs of the zodiac with the deepest appreciation for beauty. She is associated with the letter Daleth, which means a door, and also relates to the planet Venus.

Notice that she rests upon a pillow-laden throne, indicating comfort and luxury. Her white gown, although symbolic of purity is covered with fruit, indicating her own fruitfulness. It is by no mistake that the fruit that adorns her gown is the apple, turning from green to a ripe red from the energy she emits.

She is woman; she will provide man the fruit of knowledge, just as Eve did.

The Empress vibrates to the Number Three, the numeral symbolic of having made a successful start and beginning the work that is at hand, also indicating that frequently two become one and produce a third through motherhood.

Again, we see the waters of knowledge coursing through the Tarot Deck as a lush waterfall cascades behind The Empress.

When The Empress appears in a spread, she can represent an individual, a mother, usually, or also the onset of a marriage or serious relationship. She is fertile, and guards her upcoming harvest with all of her feminine powers. She is all that represents the power of the female and the pleasures inherent to the female gender.

Think of the qualities of "Mother Nature" in regard to interpreting The Empress. She can represent a specific individual, or the feminine characteristics stated above becoming active within the Querent themselves.

Since The Empress is associated with fertility, it can be assumed that her appearance in a spread denotes a relationship that is physical in nature, unless she is representative of the Querent's mother.

She can also represent the wife of a male you may be reading.

In relationship matters, The Empress represents true commitment even to the level of marriage.

In other matters, this card will indicate a mastery of a situation through traditionally feminine means, such as nurturing and creativity. She can also foretell of pregnancy and childbirth.

The positive energies of this card indicate a fertile time in the Querent's life, any plans put into action are sure to reap a generous harvest. The negative vibration of this card will indicate a person who may seek to dominate a person or situation through the use of feminine wiles.

To divine the intentions of another when this card is prevalent, they will be willing to contribute actively and creatively to make a situation work out in the favor of the Querent.

The Emperor

The Emperor, the male archetype of authority, control and power. All that is masculine, this is The Emperor. He sits upon his throne and views all that he commands and he commands all that he views.

His jeweled crown represents a clear and rich intellect and a stable position in life. He wears armor beneath his red cloak, the armor indicating his level of defensiveness; he is holding things in just as firmly as he is keeping them out. The red cloak symbolic of his passion for authority.

He rests upon a stone throne adorned with the Arian symbol of The Ram, as he is ruled by Aries. The hard cold throne he perches upon gives you an idea of his stern authority, he is unemotional and domineering.

His scepter is similar to the Ankh, for his is a passion for life. The mountains behind are symbolic of his stability, while the waters of knowledge flow by at their base.

The Emperor is ruled by the Number Four and is attributed to the letter Tzaddi.

The Emperor corresponds to the sign of Aries; he is fiery and self-centered and seeks to have his own way in all things.

The Emperor can be representative of a father figure, a husband or a male significant other, and in his best attitude, he represents stability, leadership, action, power and truth. When his negative aspects are at work, he can be a despot, behaving immaturely when his own needs are not immediately satisfied. The Emperor usually seeks to rule justly and fairly and attends to the needs of those whom he is responsible for.

When he appears in a spread, there is a significant male influence involved in the reading. Look for the person who is trying to dominate the situation under analysis, the individual does not necessarily have to be male, but will be exhibiting the male traits historically associated with patriarchal rulership.

When The Emperor is active in a spread, do not try to negotiate or manipulate him, he will see right through it and he will become angry and warlike.

The Emperor will respond to feminine energy, however, so it is safe to inform him as to how you feel and what you "do not" want versus demanding what you "do want" and telling him, what he should think and do.

In relationship matters, The Emperor represents a strong masculine energy that can be outright domineering.

In other matters, this card will indicate firm control of a situation. A person will be unyielding in pursuing their aspirations.

To divine the intentions of another when this card is prevalent, they will aggressively seek to dominate a situation.

The Hierophant

The Hierophant is our spiritual mentor. His crown and staff symbolize the spiritual and earthly planes of existence. The crosses he bears on his robe impart his divinity. At his feet lie the keys to esoteric knowledge; hidden from the mainstream, those who seek the knowledge shall be educated once the Hierophant unlocks the secrets.

Again, we see a figure seated between two pillars, symbolizing stability. The Hierophant's red robe depicts a passion for knowledge; his white undergarment and the white trim on his robe show his underlying purity.

The two monks or seekers of knowledge in the foreground come to the great teacher to learn. Their yoke shaped vestments symbolize the yoke of the oxen, as Taurus rules this spiritual card.

The Hierophant is referred to the letter Vau, and the Number Five, it is the midpoint of the journey enroute to the ten in numerology. Vau translates to the word "nail", and The Hierophant's Crown hosts three nails, holding together the spiritual and the physical realms. The three nails also are representative of the Holy Trilogy of The Father, The Son and The Holy Ghost.

The Hierophant is a teacher, a meditator, and a scholar who is well versed in that which is secret and hidden.

The Hierophant holds in much of his knowledge and seeks an inner peace through education and meditation. The Hierophant seeks to solve problems either through receiving or extending Karmic lessons.

When The Hierophant appears in a spread, someone in the situation is going to play the role of teacher, or the situation itself is a life lesson. The Querent themselves may be assuming the role of teacher, look inside the spread for indications as to what the lesson proffered may be and use your intuition to determine who is assuming the role of the educator and who the student may be.

In relationship matters, The Hierophant indicates honesty and a sense of bonding that goes beyond the physical realm into that of the spiritual, often indicating soul lessons to be shared between the pair.

In other matters, this card will indicate full disclosure of all knowledge of a situation, an honest relaying of all of the facts surrounding the circumstance at hand.

The positive energies of this card indicate a sense of honesty and guidance. The negative vibration of this card will indicate a person willing to use knowledge purely for their own benefit.

To divine the intentions of another when this card is prevalent, they will be open and honest and share all available details with the Querent concerning the matter at hand. There is a complete lack of deception when this card is present in a spread.

The Lovers

The sixth card of the Major Arcana is The Lovers, a card rich in symbolism and deep in Biblical meaning. Which traditional Bible story does the artwork on this card put you in mind of? Might it be the story of Genesis, Adam and Eve and The Garden of Eden?

The angel of God above the man and the woman motioning as to how the one soul has now been split into two, the anima and the animus, forever searching to merge into one whole spiritual being again. Twin souls, if you will, Soul Mates.

Eve seeks spiritual guidance as she looks up to the angel, the serpent, symbolizing wisdom and temptation is wrapped about the Tree of Knowledge behind her. Adam looks to Eve, awaiting her action so he can have an opposite but equal reaction, the Tree of Life ablaze with the male energy of fire behind him. The roots of the trees, Knowledge and Life, are still intertwined and the mountain in the background shows the challenges between the souls before they can reunite in spiritual bliss.

The Number Six rules The Lovers and it is associated with the astrological sign of Gemini, The Twins.

The Hebrew letter for this card is Zain, which means sword, which can swiftly dissect something into two pieces, be it a future decision, a relationship, or a personality.

The Lovers appearing in a spread can have many different and complex meanings, many times the meaning must be directly associated with the subject the Querent is addressing. The Lovers always means that there is a choice to be made, it can be a choice between lovers, or between two different paths, it can denote a choice between a moral love and a profane love, it can quite literally mean a "love affair". The cards surrounding this complex card must be carefully examined.

The Lovers are represented by a male and female figure, naked before God, just as Adam and Eve were while in The Garden of Eden. Their choice to eat of The Tree of Knowledge made them know the difference between good and evil, and this card always indicates that a choice must be made; the Querent has come to a fork in the road and must choose which path to take.

Gemini, the sign of the twins, rules this card, and rightly so. It can be said that the male and female figure represent a twin soul that has split into its male and female halves, to be cast into the Karmic Cycle, forever searching to reunite. Dual in nature this complex and legend-ridden card must be seen as a dominant force in any spread, and it can at times represent the discovery of a soul mate, which is never an easy relationship.

Contemplate on what true lovers mean to you. Where do they begin and end? What holds them together? What keeps them apart? Soul mates are often subject to high drama and difficult situations as they have much Karma from multiple lives together to resolve before they can once again become whole, become one. Their choices will determine whether they can have the relief only each other's arms can provide, the love in each other's hearts, and the contentedness they know they will find in each other's souls. Think of Romeo and Juliet, Rhett and Scarlett, Casablanca, Wuthering Heights, all difficult relationships that lack happy endings, yet true love just the same.

Choose carefully when The Lovers appear in a spread. Contemplate the consequences of each of your options before you move forward with your decision.

Repeat: Choose carefully.

In relationship matters, The Lovers indicate that a decision, a choice, must be made, look to the cards following the appearance of The Lovers to gain insight as to what the choice will likely be.

In other matters, this card will again indicate a choice or a decision that must be made, again, look to the following cards to gain insight.

The positive energies of this card indicate a true sense of loving emotions, but a need to choose how to act on them. The negative vibration of this card can indicate indecisiveness, a person stalled at a fork in the road for an indefinite period of time.

To divine the intentions of another when this card is prevalent, they have not yet made a decision concerning the matter at hand, they are still considering the options.

The Chariot

Expect to be hurled forward to your fate with sudden and sure swiftness, veering down the path trying to reign in forces that are propelling you forward at breakneck speed when The Chariot appears in a spread. The Chariot is ruled by the Number Seven, the sign of Cancer, the element of Water and is a card of Action.

The city lies behind the charioteer; he is leaving the familiar behind and being pulled out of the comfort of his familiar surroundings on to his destiny. The charioteer wears a crown of gold, symbolic of his knowledge and courage; stars surround him, indicating this is a card of destiny. His chest plate bears a square, indicating he possesses the energy of the four elements of earth, air fire and water.

His shoulder plates show the different faces of the Moon, one grimacing and the other smirking. The dragel that adorns his chariot shows that his fate is spinning while the wings above indicate speed.

The sphinxes, displaying both male and female characteristics indicate the two opposing fates, yin and yang, one countenance worried, the other sedate.

You are the Charioteer and must take control of your fate, although you may feel that the Chariot is whisking you headlong into your destiny, you must assume mental control of the vehicle.

The Chariot may have you pulled in two directions at one time, exert your mental control and decide which path will lead you to the proper destiny. The element of water rules over your subconscious, the moon, which rules Cancer, also rules that part of our psyche which is hidden, embrace the fear you may feel when careening to your destiny and you may find that it is the proper destination.

The Hebraic alphabetic association of this card is extremely complex and ties directly to the word of the Aeon, Abrahadabra, and must be associated with change.

In relationship matters, The Chariot indicates the pair rushing forward into the future at breakneck speed. A sense of urgency exists within the pair to be together and build a future, regardless of what obstacles may be present. This card can also indicate that one member of the pair is trying to maintain two simultaneous relationships at a high level of commitment, as in a married individual who cannot leave the marriage, but wishes to maintain a full blown relationship with another partner as well.

In other matters, this card will indicate a sense of urgency and movement forward, whether one is ready to move forward or not.

The positive energies of this card indicate a determination to succeed and control forces that others may perceive as insurmountable obstacles. There is a courageous energy in this card. The negative vibration of this card will indicate a person feeling that they have no control and that they are being pulled in two opposite directions at the same time with force that they may perceive as unbearable.

To divine the intentions of another when this card is prevalent, they will assertively support your cause or intention.

Strength

The Major Arcana card ruled by the Number Eight is Strength. Strength to control our animal nature and instincts and rise above them to that which is human and humane is the strength communicated in this card. Some decks entitle this card Lust, and refer to the ability to control that lust at a higher level as the divinatory message of this card.

This card is ruled by the astrological sign of Leo; the lion in the picture above is tamed by the woman's hand, when this card appears in a spread think of the quiet taming of the lion with the gentle stroke of the human hand. The woman is pictured in a white robe, symbolic of purity. She is crowned with the infinity symbol, showing knowledge of all things. She appears to be prosperous as indicated by the lush vegetation that surrounds her.

The lion submits to the woman's hand as indicated by his crouching position and the position of his tail between his legs. To prevent the lion from becoming aggressive the woman must exert and maintain her control of the beast.

Intelligence of the human vehicle tames the savage beast, whether that beast be lust, anger, or fear, we have within the strength and ability to calm, tame and domesticate the beast within us all.

The element of fire rules this card, as does the sun. This card is attributed to the Hebrew letter Teth, which means serpent. In some interpretations, we can replace the lion above with the symbol of the lion-serpent, again the fabled temptation of the female to gain the knowledge of good and evil, but the female gains the knowledge in this card and uses that knowledge to her own benefit.

When this card appears in a spread, think of the beasts within the Querent that may need to be tamed.

In relationship matters, Strength indicates a sense of fidelity and loyalty.

In other matters, this card will indicate power and success.

The positive energies of this are truth, honesty, commitment and courage. The negative vibration of this card will indicate a sense of stubbornness and an inability to negotiate.

To divine the intentions of another when this card is prevalent, they will maintain a steadfast position of support or opposition, look to the cards following in the spread to determine which position they will hold.

The Hermit

The Hermit may well be one of the most misunderstood and misinterpreted cards of the Tarot Deck.

Although the image of the solitary figure evokes a sense of loneliness, The Hermit holds a light up to show the way to our searching souls. His white hair and beard indicate that he has experience, and from that experience, he possesses knowledge and wisdom. He rests upon a yellow staff of enlightenment, and seeks to assist us in attaining the same.

The Hermit is ruled by the Number Nine and is associated with the sign of Virgo, and the Hebrew letter Yod, which means "The Hand". The letter Yod is the foundation of the Hebraic alphabet.

The Hermit symbolizes wisdom and contemplative commitment. Many think of The Hermit as a time of enforced isolation, which it can be, but most often the Querent experiencing the influence of The Hermit is simply taking a wise and quiet pause before committing to the path before them.

Do not fear The Hermit, embrace him and the solitude required to make up your mind before proceeding on your journey. Put a light on in the window if The Hermit symbolizes a loved one that is taking a sabbatical from your relationship, as they will return with renewed commitment and understanding of the relationship, as will you, if you are experiencing the meditative influence of this powerful card.

Peace, introspection, a quiet decision making time, are represented by The Hermit. Some decisions must be made alone, and once made, become a firm and established commitment, as The Hermit is now sure he has chosen the right path.

The Hermit will also indicate that the person you are inquiring about, or you yourself, is refraining from socializing during this period. Do not fear that a loved one has found a new interest if you should see The Hermit in a spread, this does indicate a period of solitude.

In relationship matters, The Hermit indicates a time of separation. This may not be a purely physical absence, but an absence of energy when the partner remains physically present. A need for solitude and thought is at hand for one or both partners, and one is best served by giving or taking the space and time needed for said reflection.

In other matters, this card will indicate a solitary time where either the Querent or the individual being inquired about needs to be alone.

The positive energies of this card indicate a newfound sense of wisdom can be gained through isolation and thought. The negative vibration of this card can indicate a person who becomes introverted to the point of antisocialism.

To divine the intentions of another when this card is prevalent, they will choose to be alone to think matters over.

The Wheel of Fortune

O h how the Karmic Wheel spins in this lifetime, in the last, and in the next. At times it spins so that we feel dizzy and disoriented, you can be sure that when this card appears in a spread that fate is about to give the wheel another turn. Luck may change for the better or worse, but change it will, and nothing you do will stop the force of the wheel, it must come to rest on its own, once the cycle has come to an end.

The Number Ten and the planet Jupiter rule The Wheel. Jupiter is the ruler of luck, The Wheel may or may not turn in favor of the Querent, but change is apparent, hold tight to your place on The Wheel so you have your bearings about you when the turning stops. Move with The Wheel, not against it, so it does not throw you off. Embrace change and grow, do not attempt to stagnate now for a cycle is ending as a new one begins.

The Wheel corresponds to the letter Kaph, which in turn relates to the palm of the hand, where your very DNA etches the lines of your personal fortune. The Wheel spins you into your destiny; Karma is at work here, so be ready for your lesson.

All four elements, fire, air, earth and water are at work in this card. The letters R, O, T and A appear on the wheel. They stand for the Royal Road and they also stand for Tarot. The fixed signs of the zodiac, Aquarius, (The Angel), Taurus, (The Bull), Leo (The Lion), and Scorpio (The Eagle), are represented by the four figures in the corners. The Serpent depicts sexual energy, wisdom and temptation, the Jackal has superb eyesight (foresight), and the Sphinx calmly observes as the Karmic wheel takes a turn.

When The Wheel of Fortune appears in a spread, you can be certain that change is looming on the horizon. Look to the subsequent cards that fall after The Wheel of Fortune appears to gain insight into what type of change is about to manifest, whether it be positive or negative in nature.

The Wheel of Fortune also indicates "forced change", you cannot always know what the universe has in store for you and when this powerful karmic card appears, the change will occur whether you wish for it to or not.

In relationship matters, The Wheel of Fortune represents change within the relationship, perhaps even to the point of a final separation, look to subsequent cards to determine the energy of the change.

In other matters, this card will indicate a change as well; again, look to the subsequent cards to determine what type of change is in the air.

The positive energies of this card indicate good fortune, luck and positive growth. The negative vibration of this card will indicate a person resistant to change, thus experiencing a "forced change" which may be difficult for the person to accept and adjust to.

To divine the intentions of another when this card is prevalent, they will seek to change the outcome of the situation either to your benefit or against your hopes and expectations.

If this card falls as the ultimate outcome position in a spread, draw a clarifier card to gain insight into the change.

Justice

The eleventh card of the Major Arcana is Justice. Eleven reverts back to the Number Two numerologically, and the sign of Libra, which indicates balance and rules this card. The card of Justice will indicate that a decision is being made that will be held firm to.

Lady Justice is seated between two pillars indicating stability. In her right hand, she wields a sword, symbolic of how she pierces the intellect to reach a decision, rather than utilizing her emotions. On her head rests a golden crown representing intelligence and position. The crown bears a square that is symbolic of the equanimity of the four elements of earth, air, fire and water. Her red robe denotes her passion for that which is fair, equal and balanced. In her left hand she hold the scales of justice, seeking to balance the factors involved in the decision making process in an intellectual manner.

Behind Lady Justice, a drape conceals the background, perhaps there are factors behind this drape that the Querent is unaware of, but Lady Justice is. She wears slippers of white, she does not dirty her feet in the mundane, but looks to larger issues. She sits upon a stone throne in order to maintain the alert attitude she must exert to make wise decisions.

Justice is the feminine compliment to The Fool, as we reached The Wheel of Fortune we completed the first cycle of our journey through the Major Arcana as ten translates back to one. The journey begins on the next level with the card of Justice, having learned the lessons of the eleven first Major Arcana; The Fool is now a bit wiser and has more of a sense of right and wrong, just and unjust.

When Justice appears in a spread you can be sure that a decision is being considered in a very serious manner and that decision is going to be presented to you in the cards that fall subsequent to the card of Justice in the spread.

The subsequent cards will give you an indication of what decision will be reached concerning the matter at hand and you can be sure that all factors have been weighed and measured by the individual responsible for making the decision in question.

If Justice appears as an outcome card in a spread it will indicate that the decision making process has not yet been completed and all factors are still under consideration.

In relationship matters, Justice represents a need for balance and consideration of each partner's viewpoints. This card can also indicate a pending divorce.

In other matters, this card will indicate a need for a decision to be made.

The positive energies of this card indicate an atmosphere of equality and balance. The negative vibration of this card can indicate a person becoming judgmental.

To divine the intentions of another when this card is prevalent, they will seek to reach a fair and balanced decision.

The Hanged Man

Time in suspension, nothing to do but "hang around" and wait. When the influence of The Hanged Man becomes apparent, it is as if the situation is in suspended animation. Stagnation, inaction, and inability to affect change occur when this card is at work.

The Hanged Man's head emanates a halo of yellow, illumination, inspiration and enlightenment. Have you ever looked at something from a different angle to change your perspective? The Hanged Man does just this while he is waiting for a situation to become mobile again.

He is bound by one foot, suspended from an apparently living and fertile tree bow. His countenance does not appear to hold expression of distress and his body position, although one would think it would be extremely uncomfortable, appears graceful in its suspension.

His tunic of blue denotes purity, purity due to the fact that he cannot currently take any action whatsoever to affect this situation. His legs bear red tights, symbolic of his passion to take action once he is released from his suspension.

When a Querent is affected by this influence, his will is surrendered and sacrificed to the will of others. For the duration of this cards' influence, the Querent cannot influence the situation at hand and is forced to endure the will of others.

The Number Twelve translates back to the Number Three, and this card is associated with that number as well as the planet Neptune and the astrological sign of Pisces. The element of water is at work here and one should let the influence of the element wash over them until the influence has passed, surrender to the water, as no amount of struggling against the tide will stop the force of the current.

Beware of escapism during this time as Neptune's influence may tempt one to live in a fantasy world while motion is suspended rather than studying the situation so that when you again are set in motion you act in the proper manner.

Use this time to observe, plan and learn.

The Hebraic letter Mem is associated with this card, Mem stands for water; tread in these waters until the tide turns in your favor when this card appears.

In relationship matters, The Hanged Man represents a time of delays and stagnation, possibly a separation as well. There will be no change or progress in the relationship until the influence of this card has passed, one or both partners may be considering the relationship from a new perspective.

In other matters, this card will indicate delays and an extended waiting period is likely before further insight can be gained.

The positive energies of this card indicate patience and the ability to gain a new perspective. The negative vibration of this card will indicate a person unwilling to make changes or consider an alternate viewpoint.

To divine the intentions of another when this card is prevalent, they will seek to slow progress toward a goal.

Death

Do not fear this card for it is not a literal death that is communicated through its' appearance, but figurative. In order for a new cycle to begin the old one must end, and end it does when the card of Death appears in a spread.

Death is a glorious card because it symbolizes that the Querent has completed a major portion of their journey and is ready for a rebirth, a new beginning. Whenever Death appears, it is a herald of a new and exciting time of fresh starts and new opportunities.

Death enters onto the scene on a white horse, at a slow pace, almost a march. He is skeletal in nature, he has shed his earthly countenance and is but a shell of what he once was, yet he wears a suit of black armor to protect himself.

He is the card that hosts the Number Thirteen of the Major Arcana, Thirteen being a holy number as it was the number of participants who took part in The Last Supper of Jesus Christ.

He is passing through the scene of the death of a king or nobleman. The young girl in the foreground, blood upon her hands, turns away from Death, perhaps she is afraid of change, but the young boy, perhaps heir to the throne looks up at death in awe, perhaps realizing the profound change that death is bringing upon him personally.

The Bishop is praying for the dead king as the sun sets on the horizon, or is it rising? The end of one era and the beginning of another occur at the same instant. The sun is pictured between two pillars, the pillars representing stability and constancy, the only thing constant in life is change.

Think of the phrase "The King is dead! Long live the King!" when this card appears in a spread. When this card influences a Querent, you must divine what is ending and what is beginning. Focus on the positive, the challenge of the new beginning, not the mourning of the loss for what once was, as it can be no more.

The Number Thirteen, which converts to Four, is associated with this card, as is the sign of Scorpio, transformation, the element of water. To wade in the waters of Death is to lose your fear of endings and to harvest the hope of a new beginning.

This card is associated with the letter Nun, or fish, life in water, the element which rules this card. Water symbolizes the subconscious activity that goes on within us all at all times, experiencing Death is to be born again.

The card of Death announces change, drastic and final.

In relationship matters, Death can represent the conclusion of a relationship; however, it more frequently indicates a change. If coupled with the card of The Tower, it will denote a sudden and unexpected breakup with little chance of reconciliation.

In other matters, this card will indicate an ending of an era, a change to the status quo.

The positive energies of this card indicate a new beginning, progress and growth. The negative vibration of this card will indicate a sense of loss as one may have difficulty in adapting to the change.

To divine the intentions of another when this card is prevalent, they will seek to bring a matter to a close.

Temperance

T emperance, ruled by the Number Five, (fourteen converted numerologically), is the alchemical card of The Major Arcana. The waters of knowledge pass freely back and forth between the cups in the Angel Michaels' hands. Michael symbolizes the sun and fire and the sign of Sagittarius rules this card, the last of the fire signs on the astrological wheel. In this card, the element of fire is in its highest form, and this card depicts the higher self, the ability to equalize and harmonize.

Michael has the name Jehovah on his robe in Hebraic letters, and Michael is the spirit of fire. He appears to have traveled from the sun itself down the long path to the waters of knowledge he is working with. His wings, with their red color and expansiveness bring to mind the power and energy of fire. His third eye is active and energy is emanating from his head depicting the power he possesses. A triangle, symbolic of the Holy Trinity and the energy that is carried spiritually with that number rests within a square, symbolic of the four elements, upon the center of his chest. Michael is the spiritually developed magician, again manipulating the four elements, but adding the element of spirit to his efforts.

He maintains perfect balance while he works with one foot in the water and one foot on the earth. The influence of this card appearing in a spread is one of harmonizing, equality and patience.

When Temperance appears in a spread concerning relationships, a happy and equitable balance has been attained. The relationship is healthy and respectful; self-control, patience and the ability to adjust exist. Balance is maintained and cultivated.

A caution for Temperance can indicate that there is a lack of control, especially when cards surrounding bring out the negative intonations of this card.

Temperance appearing in a spread where the surrounding cards are not totally positive may indicate a caution to the Querent to exhibit self-control in these matters and refrain from excessive behavior.

In relationship matters, Temperance indicates an energy of patience and cooperativeness, couples will have these qualities and the ability to work through any challenges they may be faced with.

In other matters, this card will indicate a calm and patient approach to resolving the issue at hand; knowledge will be sought and applied justly.

The positive energies of this card indicate a high level of tolerance and understanding exist. The negative vibration of this card will indicate a person who is out of control and may well be having issues with maintaining sobriety as well.

To divine the intentions of another when this card is prevalent, they will seek and provide enlightened guidance.

The Devil

The Devil, ruled by the Number Six, (fifteen converted numerologically), is the opposite of the card of Strength. In Strength we learn to control our animal natures, in The Devil, we are enslaved by them. See the male and female chained together by their animal desires, they are not interacting on a higher evolutionary plane, but are behaving as animals toward one another. Using each other in a base and profane manner, unable to rise above their own greed and need for satisfaction.

The Devil brings out our materialistic greed, deception, ill use of what talent we may possess, entrapped by earthly desires rather than freed by focusing on the higher good and the best for all. He is greed, desire, lust and surrender to animal nature.

The Devil is ruled by the sign of Capricorn, the goat, and as all cards have a positive and negative influence, so does The Devil. The Devil can signify a commitment, almost to the point of enslavement, and the card is a caution that the Querent is too committed in some area of their life, to the point that other areas of their development are neglected, such would be the interpretation should the card appear and reflect a workaholic personality.

The Devil is an illusionist. When he appears in a spread, cut through the veil of illusion and try to decipher things as they really are, not just as they appear on the surface.

The Devil is associated with the Hebraic letter 'Ayin, an eye, The Devil sees what we do not want to see, and shows you only that which he wishes you to see.

When The Devil is present in a spread it will indicate difficulties of some sort to be sure yet it can also indicate that individuals involved are not yet ready to walk away from the situation, they will stay and work through the apparent difficulties as best they can.

The Devil will indicate a strong likelihood of negative human emotions surfacing concerning the matter at hand and must be considered seriously so as not to cause irreparable damage.

In relationship matters, The Devil represents a bond that will not be broken, regardless of how difficult the relationship is.

In other matters, this card will indicate a sense of entrapment and inability to change.

The positive energies of this card indicate commitment, a willingness to do the work required to improve a situation. The negative vibration of this card will indicate a sense of bondage and enslavement. This card can also be indicative of an addictive personality.

To divine the intentions of another when this card is prevalent, they will seek an outcome that will be in their best interest only and not consider the effects of their actions upon others who may be involved.

The Tower

The Tower, malevolent and daunting, the most destructive energy within the Tarot Deck. The Tower indicates complete and utter destruction of things as they are, annihilation of the world as you know it. All is lost to the terrific and terrible force with which The Tower affects the Querent's life. Complete chaos will ensue when The Tower is active in your life.

Unlike Death, which paves the way for rebirth, The Tower is a card of total obliteration. A Karmic card in nature, the changes inherent to the card are never expected and can be catastrophic in nature, like the carnage left behind after the terrorist attack on the Twin Towers in New York City on that fateful September day in 2001. The images from that horrible day are seen in this card.

Unpredictable and merciless, The Tower is ruled by the planet Mars and the element of fire. The Hebraic letter Pe', mouth, is associated with this card, perhaps it is the great Karmic mouth swallowing up life as we know it like a nightmarish vision. One must be strong to work through the influences of The Tower.

With endings come new beginnings, so it is with The Tower, however, the new beginnings are a more difficult venture under the influence of this card, as one must literally begin from zero again, as all has been lost. The challenge is to hold fast to the faith that you can survive and thrive once The Tower has affected you.

The Tower is ruled by the Number Seven, (sixteen converted to seven as per numerology), this seven brings enlightenment through annihilation. We realize that nothing in life is permanent, and anything and anyone can change with sudden fury.

Ruled by Mars, The Tower is under the warlike influence of Aries.

When The Tower is active in a spread an ending to a situation is at hand.

In relationship matters, The Tower represents unexpected, explosive and dramatic endings. Intense quarrels and perhaps even physical violence may occur. A complete and final ending to the relationship is possible under the influence of this painful card.

In other matters, this card will indicate a destructive and chaotic force bringing about a bad ending.

The positive energies of this card indicate a clean slate with which to begin to build again. The negative vibration of this card will indicate a catastrophic and unexpected event.

To divine the intentions of another when this card is prevalent, they will seek to undermine and destroy that which one has built or is trying to build.

The Star

The Star is one of the most positive cards of the Major Arcana. It represents the ever-hopeful human spirit. The Star is ruled by the sign of Aquarius, the truth seeker, the pouring of knowledge out to mankind. When The Star appears in a spread, the Querent can rest assured that there is hope for a new and better life. The Star is an eternal optimist and can only be said to renew and discover depths of human spirit that The Devil and The Tower seek to challenge.

The Star is associated with the Hebraic letter He' and is ruled by the element of air. Enlightenment and inspiration occur when the influence of The Star hit us. Knowledge is power and the Aquarian archetype depicted on the cards shares that knowledge with mankind in the pools of the collective unconscious.

The Number Eight, (seventeen converted numerologically), rules the card of The Star. Eight stars are in the sky shining down upon the water bearer. She pours the waters of knowledge out from her pitcher into the collective unconscious.

She appears peaceful and calm in her solitude, the Tree of Knowledge appears in the distant background where a bird rests exemplifying the element of air in the card.

The soul is nearing the completion of one cycle of learning and takes pause to reflect on where one has come from prior to moving forward into a better situation.

When The Star appears, hope springs eternal.

Whenever you see The Star active in a spread optimism abounds. This card indicates that recognition will be achieved by the seeker and there is a renewed faith in the future for all involved.

In relationship matters, The Star represents optimism, growth and a true sharing of thought, emotion and physicality between the couple.

In other matters, this card will indicate a sense of hope for the future and the application of one's energies to attain these goals.

The positive energies of this card indicate a true sense of well-being that is well ingrained within the spirit. The negative vibration of this card will indicate a person who refuses to consider the negative implications of a matter, thus perhaps making a foolish decision.

To divine the intentions of another when this card is prevalent, they will provide generous support and apply themselves to assisting you in achieving your goals.

The Moon

The Moon is a complex, deep and mysterious card. The Moon is as difficult to understand as the reasons why the tides move to its rhythms and how it affects the cycles of women. When The Moon appears in a Tarot spread, you can be sure that there are things going on behind the scenes or in the Querent's own subconscious that must be affecting the situation.

The Triple Moon Goddess, representing the waxing, full and waning moons, has her eyes closed above and between the two pillars of stability, showing that even within stability; there is a cyclical rhythm of change. A dog and a wolf, representing both the tame and wild sides of our nature both acknowledge her presence, indicating that we can balance our emotions. A crayfish rises from the waters indicating the secrets beneath the surface of the water, much like our subconscious thoughts.

A path leads from the water to the mountains under the light of The Moon; do we dare to travel at night?

This card is not easy to interpret as it can indicate moodiness, deception, depression or a deep and abiding emotional tie. The Moon can also refer to cycles, cycles in life, in relationships, in time and so forth. The Moon can also refer to psychic impressions, intuition, and the feminine part of our psyche. The Reader must contemplate the entire spread in order to pull the correct application from this esoterically rich card.

The Moon is ruled by the sign of Pisces and vibrates to the Number Nine, as we convert eighteen to its numerological base. The waters of the zodiac all vibrate to The Moon's influence, but Pisces is the most developed of the watery trine and denotes the creativity, illusion, affection, martyrdom and sympathy that the influence of The Moon can stimulate. The Reader may well advise the Querent to pay close attention to their dreams during the influence of this card as the subconscious may well be trying to force information into the conscious realm of thought.

The Hebraic letter Qoph is associated with this card, and again refers to Pisces. Remember that Pisces is the last stage of winter, and perhaps at times the last stage of development of the soul. Once the lesson of the twelfth sign has been mastered, the soul has evolved through the lessons of the zodiac, The Moon rules over these lessons with its cycles. Look for the life lesson in the spread when The Moon appears.

In relationship matters, The Moon represents deep and abiding emotions, a sense of commitment, but also a sense of deep concern for the partners. There can well be hidden influences within the relationship, perhaps even to the point of dishonesty. A sense of sadness can be sensed within one, or both, of the partners and may be in existence when this card is active in a spread.

In other matters, this card will indicate moodiness and perhaps even a depressive state. A person needs to tap into their subconscious in order to gain relief from the depressiveness of this card.

The positive energies of this card indicate loving concern and a desire to nurture and heal. The negative vibration of this card will indicate a person allowing a depressive disposition to overtake their life.

To divine the intentions of another when this card is prevalent, they will be secretive and possibly dishonest. They are likely to conceal their true feelings and intentions, as they may be displeased with your desired course of action.

The Sun

The opposing energy to The Moon is The Sun. The Sun is entirely masculine in nature. Leo, a fire sign, rules the card of The Sun. The element of fire is at its most magnificent in the card of The Sun.

A golden-haired youngster, celebrating youth, rides in the nude, bareback, on a white horse. The color of the horse indicates purity, as does the nakedness of the child, unashamed the child rides in the bright sunlight, everything is out in the open enjoying the warmth of The Sun. The child waves a red banner showing passion and enthusiasm for life. The arms are spread wide open, embracing the day and indicating complete trust and faith in the security and safety of the perch upon the horse. Five sunflowers atop a garden wall greet the child in passing. All is well; nothing is hidden as in the card of The Moon, but out in the open for all to see and to share in a joyous spirit.

When The Sun appears in a spread, it is a very positive and powerful force. It shines with its fiery light on all the cards around it, blessing the Querent with vitality, energy, achievement, truth, prosperity and happiness.

Recognition abounds when The Sun shines. As with the sign of Leo, the recipient should step into the spotlight and revel in the warmth of The Sun.

Caution the Querent to be wary of arrogance, wasted energy, egotism and rash judgments when this card appears in a spread, as the confidence that The Sun brings can vibrate to these negative attributes.

The Sun vibrates to the Number One and all that confidence, energy and pride must be harnessed and used for the good of the Querent.

The Sun does indicate that good news is afoot so have your Querent use this positive time to focus these energies on their aspirations; goals are highly likely to be achieved.

The ancient Hebraic representation of this card refers to Heru-ra-ha, the Lord of the New Aeon. This interpretation of the card has it stand for Light, Life, Liberty and Love.

In relationship matters, The Sun represents a time of warmth, open affection and true love. There is a definitive desire to have the relationship in the spotlight, the couple wishes to share their happiness with the world.

In other matters, this card will indicate a time of success and acclamation.

The positive energies of this card indicate affection, attention and success. The negative vibration of this card will indicate a person who may become egotistical if care is not taken to exercise humility.

To divine the intentions of another when this card is prevalent, they will be open, honest, caring and supportive of you.

Judgment

The card of Judgment is a foreboding card. Symbolically it brings to mind the last judgment day that most modern Bible based religions refer to. All appear to be rising from the dead to meet their fate, and the interpretation of this card is quite similar.

The Angel Gabriel blows his trumpet calling all souls, the living and the dead, to meet with their fate. His purple-tinged wings show his power, his spirituality, his protective nature and his "higher" energies. Again, we see the cross that consists of four equal sides, unlike the Christian Crucifix, showing that Gabriel has mastered the elements of earth, air, fire and water, and we are being called forth to account for how well we have mastered the lessons of these elements.

When this card appears in a spread, the Querent is in a situation that may call for an examination of conscience, a grappling with faith, an awakening to the truth of a situation, or understanding. The influences of this card may cause the Querent to make major life decisions that will have long-term effects.

This card reminds us of our own mortality, and whenever we are faced with our mortality, we begin to examine our values and take stock of our lives. This card brings about this type of inner searching and reaching for the right choice.

The planet Pluto rules over this card and Pluto has direct ties to Karmic influences. If Judgment is predominate in a spread, there may be Karmic vibrations surrounding the situation, advise the Querent to make their decision with much forethought and consideration of the repercussions this decision will bring. The astrological sign of Scorpio is associated with this card through the card of Death and also through our physical death, which is also affiliated with the sign of Scorpio.

This Major Arcana is associated with the angel Heru, who is identical to the angel Hru. Hru is the Great Angel set over the Tarot and is at the Heart of the Tarot Deck.

Judgment is ruled by the Number Two in numerology and is associated with the element of water, but to the subconscious side of water more than to the emotional side.

In relationship matters, Judgment indicates that the fate of the relationship is under consideration. One partner may be considering taking the relationship to the next level or terminating the relationship, look to the surrounding cards for insight. Judgment can also indicate a rebirth of a relationship that may have been under a negative influence for some time.

In other matters, this card will indicate a far-reaching decision being made; the situation is going to change on a permanent level, for better or worse.

The positive energies of this card indicate a need to choose right over wrong, a desire to bring new life to a situation that one may have mishandled in the past. The negative vibration of this card will indicate a person willing to abandon a path as they may feel that they cannot breathe new life into a stagnant or dead situation.

To divine the intentions of another when this card is prevalent, they will seek to make a decision that will set past wrongs in the right, correcting previous errors in judgment.

The World

The World. This card represents all that is seen and unseen on the earthly plane we inhabit. Opportunities abound. There is great enjoyment and anticipation regarding life. With this card, we complete the journey of the Major Arcana. The Fool has evolved and learned all of the life lessons of the cards that lie between and now he has come into his own.

At the center of the card, we have a woman draped in a purple banner showing her power and her spirituality, she carries two wands, indicating that she has mastered the primal spiritual command of "As Above, So Below". She is surrounded by a green wreath indicating prosperity and again we see the balanced cross of the four elements of earth, air, fire and water, they encompass her as she has perfected the lessons of using them

The Water Bearer (Aquarius), the Eagle (Scorpio), the Bull (Taurus) and the Lion (Leo) adorn the four corners of the cards again, as in The Wheel of Fortune, representing the fixed signs of the zodiac and the four elements.

The World is a card of self-actualization. When we are under the influence of this card, we have reached a new plateau in our immortal development. We experience the influence of The World, completion, for a time, and then we revert back to The Fool and begin to move through our lessons once again. The cycle continues eternally until we have perfected our lessons and move on to the next level of existence.

The Hebraic letter associated with this card is Tau. When combined with the letter Beth, which applies to The Fool, it spells the word Ath; this translates to the word Essence. The World is the complement of The Fool, signifying completion of a cycle through the journey. It is the essence of life.

The World is of the element Earth, as it should be, and it is the attainment of complete understanding of earthly concerns. The World denotes victory, knowledge, fulfillment, success, opportunity and insight. The Querent should be cautioned not to allow its polar influences of materialism, mistrust, greed and stubbornness to take hold.

The World is ruled by the planet Saturn. Saturn is a stern planet whose influence is long lasting and masculine. Be grateful and appreciative for the blessings of the influence of The World or Saturn will strike you when you think that all is well. The World is ruled by the fixed signs of the zodiac, Aquarius, Leo, Taurus and Scorpio, fixed meaning immovable in this case.

Remember the Saturnine influences of discipline, time, awareness and strictness and do not interpret this card lightly. Remind the Querent that the cycle will begin again when the influence of this card has passed.

The World vibrates to the Number Three in numerology and signifies an initial completion.

In relationship matters, The World represents a couple who experiences growth, happiness and commitment.

In other matters, this card will indicate an opportunity being presented that can well change one's life in a very positive manner.

The positive energies of this card indicate prosperity, wisdom, passion and love. The negative vibration of this card will indicate a person failing to take advantage of an opportunity and thus failing to grow.

To divine the intentions of another when this card is prevalent, they will seek to clear a path to success for you.

Chapter

The Wands

Uncloaking the Tarot:

Understanding and Working Through the Suit of Wands

The Primary Influences of The Wands

The Suit of Wands refers to action being taken. It is associated with the element of fire, the south quarter of the circle, the season of spring and the time of day of noon. Typically, a Wand appearing in a spread will indicate movement or action of some kind. The Qabalah assigns the letter I from the ancient Hebraic alphabet to it. (Aries, Leo, Sagittarius).

When Wands are predominant in a spread there exists an enormous amount of energy and activity. Things are moving swiftly and rapidly. Action is sure to occur, moving the situation in a definitive direction. Movement through the suit will define the type of action that occurs.

The Wands are ruled by the element of fire, and so are thus associated with the fire signs of astrology, Aries, Leo and Sagittarius, as stated above. When the court cards appear they refer to individuals who have strong characteristics of these signs predominant in their personalities, or they may represent the influence of the element of fire on the Querent them self.

The Wands are not a silent and secretive suit, they are outspoken, they seek attention, they thrive on competition and they like to win. They have the "me first" attitude of Aries, the "look at me" attitude of Leo, and the outspoken and blunt "this is the way I see it" attitude of Sagittarius.

Negative connotations of the Suit of Wands include belligerence, self-centeredness, childishness, stubbornness and impulsive and rash behavior.

Positive influences of the Suit of Wands include bravery, ability to think quickly and act quickly, protectiveness, sincerity, valor and truth.

The Wands are associated with the season of spring. When interpreted symbolically they refer to a new beginning, the planting of seeds in fertile ground. When asking literal questions concerning timing, look to the spring months. When referring to a time of day, look to noon, when the sun, who influences all fire signs, is in his glory.

The Wands are the high noon of the Minor Arcana; they force a showdown, movement in a situation. Stagnation is not a consideration when the Wands are about. The Wands are a heroic suit when their influences are applied in a positive light, but they can be the petty villains of the deck when their negative aspects are allowed to arise.

Always caution the Querent as to the negative vibration in a spread as well as enlightening them to the positive, as all cards are polar in nature and can have influence in either direction. No one card is purely positive nor purely negative, all seventy-eight cards possess both attributes, focus on the enlightened interpretation of the cards, but always caution as to the negative influences as well.

The Ace of Wands

The Ace of Wands symbolizes fertility, male sexuality, new beginnings, swift and sudden change of course. This card begins the suit which is ruled by the element of fire, denoting action, valor, swiftness and confidence. The Ace is a healthy card and can be interpreted in several ways based upon the context of the question at hand.

All Aces are gifts from God. The artwork shows the "Hand of God" presenting the ability to take assertive action to us. We see a castle in the distance, a long journey, the gift of this Ace is the ability to do what needs to be done to embark on our journey.

In relationship readings, the Ace of Wands will indicate strong male sexual desire, aggressiveness and assertiveness. It is the physical side of a relationship, the wand pictured above being a definite phallic symbol; it can indicate pregnancy as it is the fertility of the male that is represented by the wand sprouting leaves indicating new life. The card can also represent fertility in the creative sense as well.

In readings concerning other subject matter, it denotes new beginnings, swift and at times, unexpected. The card represents the beginning of a new cycle, positive, assertive and confident.

The negative intonations of the card, or cautions, can include stubborn self-centeredness, belligerence, clinging to ones' ideas and thoughts as the only ones that are correct and refusing to act in any manner that is inclusive of another's input.

When querying another's intentions in a given situation the Ace of Wands indicates that the individual is going to take action very soon, within a brief period of time.

When asking about a time frame for an event the card indicates the first week of Spring in a long-term estimation, or for reading more immediate concerns it can indicate one day or one week, dependent upon the position in the spread.

The Two of Wands

The Two of Wands continues the enthusiasm of the Ace, however we pause to gain balance in controlling the element of fire.

A man stands on the balcony holding the world in his hand, contemplating where he needs to go, what he needs to do, and whether he shall travel alone (taking only one Wand with him), or form a partnership and take the second wand, changing one into two, on his journey.

The roses on the balcony wall form the balanced cross of earth, air, fire and water and are painted in white for purity and red for passion. Will he follow his passion or his heart?

Here is a Wand that demonstrates some restraint, as the next step on the journey is carefully considered.

The Two of Wands represents Dominion. One has a confident control over the situation and is able to steer with both the passion and the purity of fire. The Two of Wands represents the power of the individual will within the Querent.

In relationship matters, the card represents the confident continuation of the affair with the position of the card denoting who is the individual steering and guiding the pair forward.

In other matters, the card expresses consistent and confident control of the situation, balancing the matter utilizing the energy of fire through individual will.

The negative tone of this card, or caution, suggests an inability to balance oneself and a leaning toward selfishness (moving forward with only one Wand).

To divine the intentions of another, this card indicates that the person is still considering the situation, and subsequent cards will indicate the most likely outcome of that consideration.

In timing matters, the Two of Wands would indicate the second week of Spring for a long-term question, for short-range inquiries the approximate timeframe would be two days or two weeks.

The Three of Wands

The Three of Wands moves into the fiery influence of Virtue. The path of the Wands is becoming more firmly established and is workable. The stability allows the Querent to take input from others within the situation and move forward with what is in the best interest of the larger whole.

A man looks out from atop a hill, his three wands with him deciding what course is best for all involved. He is dressed in a red robe denoting his power and passion, a blue shirtsleeve shows us that his intentions are pure and the green cape over his shoulder indicates that he wishes for prosperity. The black and yellow-checkered design on his robe indicates that he is protected against negativity and is in search of enlightenment.

When interpreting this card in a divinatory spread one must always keep in mind the passion of the wands and remember that the core influence of this card is one of Virtue. This means that intentions, whatever the situation at hand may be, are pure, and that the person being inquired about truly does have the best interests of all involved at heart. It is a pensive card, not one that is likely to denote action or activity but rather a pause before decisive action is undertaken.

In relationship readings, the card will denote a workable relationship that is past the first blush of infatuation and the process of truly getting to know one another at a deeper level is at work. Things are moving forward on a healthy path of interaction and care.

In other matters, the card establishes a good foundation with which to move forward to the next level of interaction and existence. The card does not indicate hasty decisions but well thought out actions deliberate to the achievement of a goal.

The negative tone of this card can be a sense of martyrdom in that the needs of the self are set to the side in order to satisfy the needs of others. If not done with an open and giving heart and soul, moving forward to please others will cause a resentment to build within the individual and can become problematic later on. In sacrificing ones' individual needs one may actually be taking on more than one can yet bear.

To divine the intentions of another, keep in mind that again, this card denotes Virtue, so the person one is inquiring about is trying to choose the next beneficial course of action to all involved in the situation.

In timing matters, this card denotes the third week of Spring for long-term matters and indicates an approximate three day or three week period for questions pertaining to more short-term concerns.

The Four of Wands

The Four of Wands appearing in a spread is a time for celebration! Rejoice! All is well and moving forward at a successful rate. Happiness and Completion are at hand. A contentedness that things have taken off and are working well abounds.

Four Wands form an archway with a bough filled with fruit and greenery at the top bringing a sense of fruitfulness and prosperity as you gaze upon the card. Two figures, one dressed with a blue sash, indicating purity and the other with a red sash, indicating passion, are bidding a welcome and seem to be waving you in to join them.

The castle bears red domes indicating power and authority must be contained within these walls. More guests are moving toward the castle grounds in the background of the picture indicating a happy gathering is taking place.

The one word to be associated with this card is the word "Rejoice"! This is a happy card and you can be sure that glad tidings are coming your way when this card is present in a spread.

In relationship matters this card indicates a happy and true commitment being made, as represented by the pair of figures adorned in the colors of blue and red, for passion and purity, you can be sure that your partner is wanting to be exclusive to you and socialize with you as a couple presented to the outside world.

This card can also denote marriage in the broader perspective of divination.

In other matters, this card denotes a sense of well being and prosperity. Goals are being achieved and recognized and celebrated openly.

The negative tone of this card is that one may become overconfident with initial success and fail to maintain the same attentiveness to matters at hand. One must always be sure to continue to cultivate and care for our successes in relationship and career and all matters less the initial success be short-lived.

To divine the intentions of another this cards indicates that the individual in question is feeling a sense of sheer happiness and wishes to share that joy with those encountered.

In timing matters, this card will indicate the fourth week of Spring for long-term inquiries and for shorter-term questions, it will indicate an approximated period of four days or four weeks.

The Five of Wands

The Five of Wands brings the influence of Strife into a spread. There is confusion, bickering, and battling. Someone is not getting their own way and refuses to see all sides of an issue. The clinging to one's own insistence on control causes discontent and stagnation of movement. Energy is focused on arguing one's point so no progress can be made while this influence is present.

Five figures, dressed in varying colors of red (passion), yellow (enlightenment), white (purity), green (prosperity) and blue (serenity) seem to be battling amongst each other, each trying to raise his wand individually but feeling blocked by his fellows as they, too, struggle to set their wands upright. When working individually they are at cross-purposes and unable to complete their tasks.

The five figures also represent the five elements of Earth, Air, Fire, Water and Spirit. Look closely at the picture, are they truly battling for position or are they working in conjunction with each other? Are they pooling their energies, not to have their individual wands stand alone, but are they actually constructing a star? When we use our resources to assist each other, don't we end up with much better results?

Strife is the one key word to associate with this card when taken at face value.

In relationship matters, this card can indicate the struggle for dominance in a pairing. Neither party will agree to any type of compromise, nor will the relationship move forward until the matter is resolved. The pair must learn to use their energies in unison or else struggle and conflict will continue and progress cannot occur.

In other matters senseless quarrels, unnecessary stress and delays, continue until one deactivates the influence by broadening their perspective of the situation and applying a "teamwork" mentality to the matter at hand.

The positive influence of this initially negative card can be the courage to stand one's ground against adversity when necessary. The most well dignified interpretation of this card is the ability to work together within a situation in order to achieve the desired goal.

To divine the intentions of another when this card appears one must be aware of a sense of resistance within the individual. An uncooperative attitude will exist.

In timing matters look to the fifth week of Spring for long-term inquiries and for shorter-term concerns, this card indicates either five days or five weeks.

The Six of Wands

The Six of Wands removes us from the struggle of the Five and we move into the influence of Victory! We have successfully completed the first part of our journey through the Wands and have brought our egos under mature control. We no longer require the attention and acclaim we longed for as infants of the suit, but move to a mature and self-confident stage.

In studying the card, we see what appears to be a victorious and triumphant appearance or return. The wreath atop the wand carried by the rider, as well as the wreath that he wears upon his head, indicates completion. The traveler has come to a place of success. He has successfully absorbed the lessons of the One, Two, Three, Four and Five of Wands and he is ready to move higher in his journey through the Wands.

The white horse he rides is facing forward, indicating forward momentum and growth. The horse bears a green blanket indicating prosperity and well-being. The rider wears conservative clothes showing that he is humble in appearance, ready to travel further but pausing to measure his success thus far. He is welcomed by his peers as he rides through the crowd.

Victory is the energy that this card indicates.

In relationship matters, this card indicates that the querent will achieve their desired goals. It also indicates that the querent is being appreciated by their partner or potential mate. The querent will experience success in the relationship itself.

In other matters expect that you will arise victorious. Obstacles will, or have been, overcome and success is at hand. Our wishes are granted and we enjoy success, recognition and attention.

The negative tone of this card can be an overconfidence that overrides common sense making our victory short-lived and our success shallow.

In matters of timing this card will indicate the sixth week of Spring for long-term concerns, for short-term inquiries this card indicates either six days or six weeks.

The Seven of Wands

The Seven of Wands brings us under the influence of Valor. We are brave and courageous in the face of competition. We hold our own and stand our ground against adversity. We are strong.

A figure stands at the edge of a precipice holding his Wand in a defensive posture. Six Wands are approaching him. Are they a threat? One would certainly assume so by glancing at the card. His feet are firmly planted and he is ready for battle if it is necessary.

He wears the colors of green and yellow, prosperity and enlightenment are his energies and he may need to defend those energies when this card is active in a spread. Perhaps one of the bearers of the other six Wands wishes to usurp his position at the top of the hill?

Valor is the energy most frequently associated with this card. Courage is likely to be required when this energy is present.

In relationship readings, this card suggests that there is competition for the affections of our intended or our current partner. Someone else has an interest in the object of our affections and desires their attention. We cannot allow this to undermine our own sense of enlightenment and happiness, yet we must be alert to any complications that may arise from such a situation.

In other matters, this card refers to stiff competition that requires us to be steadfast in our hold over a situation. We must be aware that if allowed, others would certainly take our place gladly, so we must be vigilant in defending what is perceived to be ours.

The negative intonation of this card can indicate the inability to face competition and a weakening of the will. The card can indicate surrender if one does not maintain one's standards.

To divine the intentions of another when this card is present you must consider that there are outside influences attempting to draw their attention away from their connection to you. It can also indicate that the person you are inquiring about has every intention of competing with you to try to take away what is already yours, whether it be a relationship, a belonging, a job or an object, this person desires what you have.

In timing matters, this card will indicate the seventh week of Spring for long-term concerns and it will indicate either seven days or seven weeks for shorter-term concerns.

The Eight of Wands

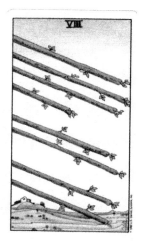

The Eight of Wands brings us back to the positive energies of the suit. The Eight indicates swiftness; messages are hurled at us unexpectedly and quickly. We barely have time to realize that this sudden change in the level of communication has taken place; the card moves us into the energy of Swiftness.

Eight Wands are pictured heading straight and sure toward their target. Many liken this image to those of Cupid's arrows approaching a target. You can be sure when this card appears that communication is imminent.

Swiftness is heralded by the appearance of this card. No longer will you have a chance for quiet contemplation as energies will have a sense of urgency about them not present in any other card in the deck.

There is no stopping the information flow from the Eight of Wands. Sudden and rapid growth of a situation occurs.

In relationship readings the card indicates messages of love coming at us when we least expect them. The messages will be swift and numerous in nature and are most often positive in intent.

In other matters, the card represents the communication lines opening enabling movement to the next stage.

The negative influence of this card can be impulsive messages sent or received that have no basis in reality or sincerity.

To divine the intentions of another when this card is present you can be sure that they are longing to communicate. They will be reaching out to you suddenly and perhaps unexpectedly.

In timing matters, this card indicates the eighth week of Spring for long-term concerns and for short-term matters look to eight days or eight weeks.

The Nine of Wands

The Nine of Wands brings us Strength. We have what it takes to move forward on our journey. We have learned the lessons of the prior pip cards and we are ready to move to the completion of the suit, the challenge that fire presents us has us weary, but yet we can go on.

A figure stands before eight wands lined up behind him representing the experiences of the prior eight cards of the suit. He holds the ninth Wand firmly, resting upon it when necessary but ready to defend the eight wands behind him if necessary.

He is battle weary, injured, but still he is ready to defend what he has learned on his journey.

In relationship readings, our connection has solidified. We have endured the pain that passion can sometimes inflict upon us and we have reveled in our victories, no matter how fleeting. We are sure of where we stand within our relationship and feel the strength that security can grant us.

In other matters, we have prepared well and the tools of the element of fire are at our disposal. We know when to be proud and when to be humble, we know how to listen to others and take them into consideration. We are not the center of the universe, but we do have the power to affect our surroundings.

The negative tone of this card can be ignoring the wisdom we have earned through experience and reverting back to less mature tactics, lacking humility and manifesting stubbornness.

To divine the intentions of another in reference to the energy of this card you can be sure that they will stand their ground. If they are a foe, they will be a worthy adversary and a battle will surely ensue, if they are a friend, they will stubbornly stand by you through good times and bad.

In timing matters look to the ninth week of Spring for long-term issues and for short-term concerns look to nine days or nine weeks.

The Ten of Wands

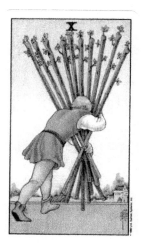

The Ten of Wands takes us under the influence of Oppression. We are burdened, but remember that we are never burdened with more than we can bear. If we have been attentive to the lessons along our paths so far, we have the knowledge and strength to effectively administer our burden and move forward on our journey.

A figure is bent over under the weight of the burden of the ten wands he is attempting to carry. He must move all ten wands forward with him in order to utilize the gifts of the wands which are masculine fertility and creativeness, dominion, virtue, joy, strife, victory, valor, swiftness, strength and oppression.

Some of the gifts of the Wands may seem to be a hard lesson to accept, but without the gifts of strife and oppression, can one truly know joy or true virtue or strength?

Oppression is the sense of being weighed down and having worked our way through the suit of Wands we may be feeling the weight of the lessons learned as we carry them forward on our journey.

In relationship readings this card can refer to the participants having much to care for and about within the context of their immediate circle. There can be others to care for, children, elderly parents, invalids or there may just be many details to juggle and work through in order to maintain the relationship. Have faith, the card's influence will pass as the cycle of the Tarot continues.

In other matters, we find that Oppression is the influence that is predominant and, again, we must use the lessons learned previously to work with our burdens and not against them.

The positive influence of this card is knowing that committing to our burdens ensures our release from them.

In timing matters look to the tenth week of Spring for long-term concerns and for short-term inquiries look to ten days or ten weeks.

The Page of Wands

PAGE of WANDS.

The Page of Wands has been released from the burden of the Ten and has found a new outlook after the trials of the Pips. He is just reaching maturity within the energy of the element of Fire and hope abounds within his breast. The Page vibrates to the influence of the Astrological Sign of Sagittarius; he is outspoken, blunt and honest to a fault. He represents the earthy part of fire, using his energy to pursue physical pleasures and material wealth.

The Page, as with all court cards in the suit of fire, is dressed in the colors of enlightenment and passion. Salamanders adorn his tunic, as they were once thought to have the ability to walk through fire, unharmed. He seems to be admiring the wand that he holds, eager to place it into action after earning the right to it through the pip cards.

The Page is eager to experience activity; he is ready for action and desires the freedom to do as he pleases. The Page is lucky and travels well amongst people and places unfamiliar to him.

The influence of this card in a relationship reading can indicate that the couple is ready to travel and experiment, and to be blatantly honest with each other. An honest energy exists between the pair when the Page of Wands appears in a spread.

In other matters, the card can indicate the need for adventure, to exercise the freedom that we all desire from time to time.

The negative tone of this card can indicate a lackadaisical attitude brought about by extensive daydreaming. One being influenced in a negative way by this card will not actively seek adventure but will only dream of it.

To divine the intentions of another when this card appears, consider that they will be brutally honest with you and wish to be socially active in some capacity in your life. A need for freedom and independence will exist in conjunction with shared experiences that can be confusing if not understood.

In timing matters, the Page of Wands will indicate the eleventh week of Spring for long-term concerns and will translate to either eleven days or eleven weeks for shorter-term matters. This card can also indicate timing occurring during the time that the Sun transits Sagittarius.

Contrary to popular interpretation, the Page of Wands is unlikely to represent a youthful individual with red hair. If the physical interpretations of the Tarot were to hold true to the depictions in the artwork on the cards, all physical descriptions would be limited to members of the Caucasian race. To truly understand the card, look to the personality and energies of the card for a description of the individual; do not try to describe physical attributes. Many traditional readers do not expand their interpretations beyond the physical.

Court cards appearing in spreads do not necessarily represent people; they may well be solely representative of the energy in a situation and not a person.

The Knight of Wands

The Knight of Wands rushes onto the scene with all the expediency expected of the suit of fire. He represents the fiery part of fire, passions that can ignite and burn brighter, or burn each other out. Leo rules the Knight of Wands, and as with all knights, he is a messenger. This messenger brings news of action, happenings, unexpected and quick.

The Knight wears the colors of the suit of fire, yellow and red, as do all court cards of the suit. Salamanders adorn his tunic as they were once thought to have the ability to walk through fire. His horse exudes the energy of the suit, swiftness and aggressiveness, a need for haste is the energy of this volatile card.

As the horse and rider are facing to the left, this card can indicate a speedy return, as when a lover has been absent and suddenly reappears more passionate than ever.

In relationships, the Knight of Wands pursues his interest relentlessly and with great speed. He rushes into the life of the intended with all the force of his fiery and assertive nature, but he can be just as quickly absent.

In relationship readings, the Knight of Wands can indicate a swift and sudden return; he will also indicate an individual that will assertively pursue your affections. He may be gone just as quickly as he arrived if he becomes bored or feels stagnant. The energy of this card can also indicate an individual who may jump to conclusions rather than taking the time to ensure understanding when conflicts arise.

In other matters, look for swift and aggressive action and movement. Any period of stagnation passes quickly and is eliminated under this Knight's influence.

The negative connotation of this card is one of impulsiveness. Use forethought.

To divine the intentions of another when this card is present you can be sure that they do not want to stop and take care of details or have lengthy conversations concerning your situation. The energy of this card indicates that they will likely make a quick appearance and disappear just as quickly unless supported by more stable cards. Individuals under the influence of this card will agree with you so that they may quickly go on their way and may fail to follow through on anything that you do agree upon.

In matters of timing look to the twelfth week of Spring and for shorter-term concerns look to twelve days or twelve weeks. This card can also indicate timing occurring during the time that the Sun transits Leo.

Contrary to popular interpretation, the Knight of Wands is unlikely to represent a young man with red hair. If the physical interpretations of the Tarot were to hold true to the depictions in the artwork on the cards, all physical descriptions would be limited to members of the Caucasian race. To truly understand the card, look to the personality and energies of the card for a description of the individual; do not try to describe physical attributes. Many traditional readers do not expand their interpretations beyond the physical.

Court cards appearing in spreads do not necessarily represent people; they may well be solely representative of the energy in a situation and not a person.

The Queen of Wands

She enjoys being Queen. She does not want any competition, she and she alone is the matriarch of the spread, and any challenges to her authority are dealt with swiftly and effectively. She is ruled by the fiery nature of Leo and must maintain the attention of her loyal subjects to remain content.

The Queen of Wands is the watery part of fire, she can be steamy and sensuous, or she can totally extinguish any thoughts of passion you may have with her arrogant bearing.

She sits upon her sun-drenched throne, a Wand for her scepter in one hand and the sunflower in her other hand. Her throne is adorned with images of the lion, as she is a pure Leonine energy through and through.

She has a volatile temper and a narcissistic insistence on doing things her way. She draws men to her by her fiery independence and strength and chooses the suitor who will best support and enhance her domain.

In relationship readings, this Queen will indicate a fiery female who will not stand for competition for the affections of her intended or her loved one. She is a woman who is straightforward and self-confident.

In other matters, the influence of this Queen will reflect an individual with this type of nature within the focus of the query or this energy manifesting within the Querent themselves.

The negative tone of this card is the egotistical feminine nature that can result in a narcissistic focus on the self rather than on the entire situation at hand.

To divine the intentions of another when this card appears in a spread be aware that the person you are inquiring about will behave in a totally self-serving manner.

In matters of timing look to the thirteenth week of Spring for long term concerns and the thirteenth day or week for shorter term concerns. This card can also indicate timing occurring during the time that the Sun transits Leo.

Contrary to popular interpretation, the Queen of Wands is unlikely to represent a woman with red hair. If the physical interpretations of the Tarot were to hold true to the depictions in the artwork on the cards, all physical descriptions would be limited to members of the Caucasian race. To truly understand the card, look to the personality and energies of the card for a description of the individual; do not try to describe physical attributes. Many traditional readers do not expand their interpretations beyond the physical.

Court cards appearing in spreads do not necessarily represent people; they may well be solely representative of the energy in a situation and not a person.

The King of Wands

The King of Wands is Aries personified. He is the King. This King is authoritarian and demanding, yet he tends to those he is responsible for with regal guidance and compassion. This King generally represents a man who is married and mature and may have a military bearing or experience.

He represents the airy part of fire, that which can be whipped into frenzy by the ideas air blows into his energetic flame.

Again, as in all the court cards of the Suit of Wands, we see the King adorned in the colors of passion and enlightenment, yellow and red. The King also bears a green collar and green shoes indicating his prosperity. Lions, representing the energy of the sign of Leo, and salamanders, once thought to be able to walk through fire, adorn his throne.

The King casts his glance to the side, indicating that he is always vigilant over what he perceives to be under his rule.

This King enjoys the beginning of new enterprises, but then usually hands them over to someone else to work out the details.

In relationship readings, he will generally represent a man who is currently or previously married and takes good care of those in his nuclear and extended family, while satisfying his own needs as he sees fit.

Although loyal to those he loves, he will not be faithful until he has found his true love, and his true love is the one who makes him feel that he is the center of the kingdom.

This man does require that his ego be stroked on a regular basis.

When this card appears in spreads relating to other matters, you are looking at a masculine energy of management being present, and you will be expected to follow through with any actions that you state you will take.

The negative tone of this card is a leaning toward childishness and selfishness from one who is mature enough to know better.

To divine the intentions of others when this card appears, be assured that you will gain the support of those in a position of authority, but you will be held accountable for your decisions.

Contrary to popular interpretation, the King of Wands is unlikely to represent a man with red hair. If the physical interpretations of the Tarot were to hold true to the depictions in the artwork on the cards, all physical descriptions would be limited to members of the Caucasian race. To truly understand the card, look to the personality and energies of the card for a description of the individual; do not try to describe physical attributes. Many traditional readers do not expand their interpretations beyond the physical.

Court cards appearing in spreads do not necessarily represent people; they may well be solely representative of the energy in a situation and not a person.

The Cups

Uncloaking the Tarot:

Understanding and Working Through the Suit of Cups

The Primary Influences of The Cups

The Suit of Cups is associated with emotion, love and human relationships, when predominant in a spread it nearly always pertains to matters of the heart. The Season of Summer, the West Quarter of the Circle, the Element of Water, the Letter O, and Dusk are associated with Cups. (Pisces, Cancer, Scorpio).

When Cups are predominant in a spread, you can be sure that the relationships and emotional life of the Querent are the primary subject matter of the spread. Emotional concerns are of primary importance and the Querent may find movement and change, for better or worse, occurring within their primary relationships.

The Cups are ruled by the element of water, and so are thus associated with the water signs of astrology, Pisces, Cancer and Scorpio, as stated above. When the court cards appear they refer to individuals who have strong characteristics of these signs predominant in their personalities, or they may represent the influence of the element of water on the Querent themselves.

The Cups are an emotive suit; they speak of love, relationships, commitment, and the hope for the same. The Cups are a gentle and feminine suit, seeking to teach the Querent the lessons of relating to those who are of primary importance in the Querent's life. They have the sympathetic attitude of Pisces, the nurturing attitude of Cancer, and the secretive and lustful attitude of Scorpio.

Negative connotations of the Suit of Cups include martyrdom, possessiveness, fantasy and emotional and unrealistic behavior.

Positive influences of the Suit of Cups include love, commitment, emotional security, serenity and familial bliss.

The Cups are associated with the season of Summer. When interpreted symbolically they refer to the summer of life, health, vitality and growth. When asking literal questions concerning timing, look to the summer months. When referring to a time of day, look to dusk, when the moon, who influences all water signs, our emotions and our subconscious, is at its strongest.

The Cups are the dusk of the Minor Arcana; they bring us to the end of our day when we seek family and friends to recharge our emotions. Material concerns and rampant activity are not a consideration when the Cups are about. The Cups are a nurturing and loving suit when their influences are applied in a positive light, but they can be the plague of self-doubt and insecurity concerning our close human connections when their negative aspects are allowed to arise.

Always caution the Querent as to the negative vibration in a spread as well as enlightening them to the positive, as all cards are polar in nature and can have influence in either direction. No one card is purely positive or purely negative, all seventy-eight cards possess both attributes, focus on the enlightened interpretation of the cards but always caution as to the negative influence as well.

The Ace of Cups

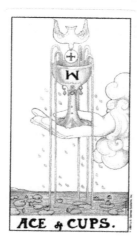

The Ace of Cups symbolizes love, female sexuality, feminine fertility, new beginnings within relationships and the swift and sudden onset of emotions. This card begins the suit which is ruled by the element of water, denoting emotion, love, commitment and desire. The Ace is a healthy card and can be interpreted in several ways based upon the context of the question at hand.

All Aces are gifts from God. The artwork shows the "Hand of God" presenting the Cup of Emotion to us. Cups are receptive, they receive love and contain it, yet this gift allows us the ability to give love fully. Five founts pour up and out of the cup representing the five elements of Earth, Air, Fire, Water and Spirit. All five elements receive this outpouring of love. A white dove appears above the cup symbolizing purity and spirit, he holds the sacred host marked with the balanced cross of the four elements above the chalice, communing the energy of the Holy Spirit with this gift from God. Divine Inspiration can be found when we allow the energy of the Ace of Cups into our lives. This card denotes creativity and fertility in action, thought, word and deed.

The picture puts one in mind of a communion chalice, as it does, in its' most spiritual sense, represent the communing of man with God.

In relationship readings, the Ace of Cups will indicate strong female sexual desire, receptivity and acceptance. It is the loving and nurturing side of a relationship, the cup being the female receptacle to the male phallic symbol of the wand. This card can indicate feminine fertility and the onset of a pregnancy, if the balance of the spread supports this interpretation. The presence of the Ace of Cups in a spread indicates genuine love and affection between the subjects of the reading.

In other matters, the Ace of Cups will represent creativity in whatever the matter at hand is. Think of the word "birth" when the Ace of Cups is well dignified in a spread.

The negative implications of this card are a blind acceptance of a situation regardless of the harm or negativity that may surround it, as in a codependent relationship where one is an enabler, or in a work situation where one is afraid to make change and allows their ideas to be usurped by others without objection.

To divine the intentions of another when the Ace of Cups appears, it is indicative of a receptive and cooperative nature, and of a wish to display affection and positive caring emotions.

In timing matters, look to a one day or one week period for short-term concerns, for longer term projections the timing would indicate the first week of Summer.

The Two of Cups

The Two of Cups continues the attraction and emotion of the Ace and brings about a reciprocation of the emotions that are at hand. It can symbolize a union, a meeting of two hearts, or a meeting of the minds. It is a positive card in nature and shows the teaming of two individuals in an emotional bond.

A couple faces each other, and exchanges their cup of emotion with each other, under the fierce and protective winged lion above. This symbolizes a spiritual, as well as an emotional union, as the lion serves as guardian of the lovers below, "What God hath put together let no man pull apart". This is one of the most clearly definable marriage cards in the Tarot. The woman is clothed in the colors of purity and pure love, white and blue; she wears red slippers of passion and is crowned by a green wreath indicating her fertility.

The man is adorned in bright yellow indicating enlightenment. His tunic bears the symbolic balanced cross that we see throughout the tarot, representing the elemental energies of earth, air, fire and water once again. All of the elements are represented in this card, creating a balance of nature, which all relationships require in order to be successful.

The Two of Cups, quite succinctly, represents Love, the blending of two into one. Each must surrender his individual will and manifest a united front to the outside world. Unity is represented by the appearance of this card in a spread.

In relationship readings, this card indicates love, commitment and becoming a true couple. When the Two of Cups appears in a relationship spread, you can be sure that no matter what the hardship or obstacle, the two will become one again. If the couple is enduring a separation, no matter what the circumstances, the Two of Cups indicates that they will merge together once more. If pondering the future likelihood of commitment in a relationship, this card bodes well for marriage potential.

In other matters, this card indicates a cooperative effort in any given situation, a partnering or an ally is sure to be present. This card also indicates face-to-face meetings when inquiring about communication.

The negative aspect of this card can be an inability to exist outside the realm of relationship as an individual, to be codependent. It can also indicate an inability to act independently and an unhealthy need to seek another's counsel on a regular basis.

To divine the intentions of another when considering this card, it indicates that the person in question does wish to merge and connect with the seeker.

In timing matters, look to two days or two weeks for short-term inquiries and for longer-term concerns look to the second week of Summer.

The Three of Cups

The Three of Cups symbolizes Abundance. One is emotionally satisfied and free to celebrate and enjoy the good feelings that a sense of emotional security brings about. The Three of Cups indicates a time of celebration and happiness, good times abound!

Three maidens raise their cups to toast their happiness. The energy from the card indicates self-confidence and pleasure. Their cups are raised high, their heads are tilted upward, they look as if they may break into a dance at any moment. The products of a happy harvest lay at their feet. The women are dressed in white, yellow and red, representing that their joy comes from purity, passion and enlightenment. They know who they are, they know what they have accomplished, and they are celebrating their satisfaction under the open sky.

In relationship matters, this card will bring about a sense of well being within the parameters of the relationship. The individuals will be engaging in social activities as a couple and will enjoy having been recognized as such. In old or new relationships, this card indicates a happy time when much socializing is upon the pair, and they are presenting themselves to the outside world as a couple.

In other matters, look for heightened social activity, dating and a sense of well being and belonging.

The negative implications of this card can be indicative of overindulgence in food, drink or sexual experience. A caution to the seeker not to excessively celebrate is well advised. This card, if ill dignified, may indicate a substance abuse issue manifesting as well.

To divine the intentions of another when considering this card, you can be sure that they will want to socialize publicly with the seeker and are looking forward to having an enjoyable time. It can also indicate an invitation to a party hosted by another.

In timing matters, look to three days or three weeks, for short-term concerns and for longer term considerations this card will indicate the third week of Summer.

The Four of Cups

In our journey into the Suit of Cups thus far, we have seen the birth of love, the successful acquisition of a partner, and a celebration of the happy times this pairing has brought to us. When we move on to the Four of Cups there is a definite change of tone.

The Four of Cups symbolizes Luxury. Perhaps the Querent has not taken caution against overindulgence seriously and now finds they are feeling as if the happiness experienced thus far in the suit is not lasting.

A young man clothed in the colors of passion, prosperity and purity sits under a tree with four cups before him. Three of the cups rest on the ground right in front of him; they represent what he already has and what he has already experienced, his present situation. In the air above them a fourth cup is being offered out of seemingly thin air, it is just above his eye level so that he is unsure of what the cup may contain. His arms are crossed in front of him in a defensive posture as he considers the scene before him. Should he continue on his current path with the three cups he is already in possession of, or should he abandon the known for the unknown, and grasp for the cup being offered out of the unknown?

When the Four of Cups appears in a spread, you can be sure that a reevaluation is underway. Someone is reevaluating the relationship or the situation at hand, prior to moving forward. It can also mean that someone under the influence of the card is considering an alternate partner, and is being tempted to stray.

In relationship readings, the Four of Cups is a time of uncertainty. A decision is going to be made whether to stay or to go. The subsequent cards in the spread will give you an indication of which path will be chosen. If The Four of Cups falls as an outcome card you will not get a definitive answer just yet, as the evaluation process is not completed, and there is not enough energy within the thought process yet to indicate which choice is more likely.

In other matters, this card again indicates a period of evaluation, and one must consider the balance of the spread in order to divine the likely outcome.

The positive tone of the Four of Cups is that this period of contemplation can lead to a deeper commitment, once all of the reflection has been completed.

The negative vibration of this card can lead to a break up or an affair outside of the primary relationship. In other matters, it can indicate being sidetracked or distracted by the consideration of new opportunities.

To divine the intentions of another when this card appears, you must take pause, as their intentions are not defined until the decision they are contemplating is reached.

In timing matters, look to four days to four weeks for a decision to be reached, for long-term considerations the timing will occur during the fourth week of Summer.

The Five of Cups

The Five of Cups brings the influence of Disappointment into a spread. One is saddened by the loss of what has been poured out from the cups that have been spilled, and one fails to appreciate what yet remains in the upright cups.

A depressive figure cloaked in black, which is the total absence of color, and indicates the absence of energy, gazes down upon three spilled cups. The feeling that comes from this card is easily felt; it is sad, depressed and despairing. The figure cannot be bothered to turn around and appreciate the two full cups that are still standing, he can only focus on what is lost, not realizing that he needs only to turn around to see that all is not lost and hope can be regained.

The melancholy vibration of this card can indicate mourning over a loss or a change. This card indicates that the subject of the reading is dwelling on the negative, and the perceived loss, and refusing to see the positive polar influence of each loss and change.

In a relationship reading, this card indicates that the person in question is not over a painful situation, that they are still in the mourning process, and not ready to move forward. It can be mourning over a breakup, or a hurt that occurs within an existing relationship. One must encourage the person to turn around and see the two full cups that remain, remind them that each change in our life brings about an opportunity for growth, that one should focus on what yet remains, and not on what one has lost.

In other matters, this card will indicate a focusing on the negative and a depressive demeanor.

The positive tone of this card is the ability to contemplate what one still has and to move forward optimistically.

To divine the intentions of another when this cards' energy is present, you can be fairly certain that they are in a passive state of sadness and not yet ready to make change, or to move forward. Clinical depression can be a possibility if the supporting cards are of a like tone, a physical examination by a medical professional may be called for.

In timing matters, look to five days or five weeks for short-term concerns and the fifth week of Summer for longer-term considerations.

The Six of Cups

After experiencing love, coupling, celebration, and then the harsher cards of reevaluation and disappointment, we return to a more positive energy in the Six of Cups, Pleasure.

The Six of Cups brings us pleasure associated with feelings of nostalgia, loves and lives gone by and perhaps forgotten, but awoken anew in the psyche of the subject.

Two young children are at play in the garden, a sense of innocence is depicted as the young boy presents the girl with a white flower, indicating purity. We see the balance of the four elements return to the card, represented by the white cross on the pedestal in the background. The children are again clothed in colors of purity, passion and enlightenment, respectively blue, red and yellow. The home in the background gives one a sense of security, the children appear safe and happy, and have a caring posture toward each other.

Pleasure in its most simple sense is indicated by this card.

In relationship readings, this card bodes well for the couple, as it brings a validation of security and happiness. It can also indicate children being produced by the pair in the future. When a relationship is undergoing a difficult period or a break up, this card indicates that Reconciliation will occur between the pair. This is a sweet and loving card and indicates that a true love exists between a pair.

The Six of Cups can also indicate the return of a love from the past, or the deep bonding that occurs between partners when they share their pleasant memories of their early years together. The sense of pleasure associated with this card is one of satisfaction and emotional well-being.

In other matters, the appearance of the Six of Cups indicates acceptance, and perhaps a shared common history. A nostalgic tone will manifest.

The negative tone of this card can be interpreted as one who is living in the past and not moving forward with life.

To divine the intentions of another when this card is active in a spread, one must consider that they yearn for something in their past, or are going to return to something in their past that is fondly thought of.

In timing matters, look to six days or six weeks for short-term inquiries and the sixth week of Summer for longer-term concerns.

The Seven of Cups

The Seven of Cups brings us out of the warm embrace of nostalgia and brings us to an atmosphere of Illusion. We may be unrealistically suspicious of our surroundings or we may be simply looking at our lives through rose-colored glasses.

The Seven of Cups brings us to a place where nothing is as it appears to be. We may fear the unknown, and since we fear, choose not to reach out and discover it. We may be projecting our image of what we wish our partner would be onto them, rather than seeing them for who they truly are.

The silhouette of a man faces seven cups that are seemingly floating in the clouds above him. These cups contain different dreams and fantasies that are common to us along our journeys. One cup contains a castle, perhaps referring to one wishing for a dream home. The next cup contains jewels, many people fantasize about wealth, and this may be a temptation currently being dwelled upon in our thoughts. A third cup presents us with a wreath, some of us long for pure power and status and may believe that power is the route to happiness.

A dragon with a distinct hue of blue to it's skin is perched upon the fourth cup. Blue is a color that denotes purity, perhaps we wish to be courageous and rescue those in distress from any implications of danger that we perceive, truly wanting to be respected as the archetypical hero.

A human head, again, blue in color, floats disembodied above the fifth cup, indicating that perhaps our road to purity, is perceived to be found through pure intellect. A lifetime of scholarly pursuit will appeal to many of us on our journey.

In the sixth cup, a figure stands alone, shrouded in white, hands outstretched to receive and surrender to the universe, a red and yellow aura emanates from the figure, symbolizing passion and enlightenment. Christians among us may find the figure to be suggestive of Jesus. We may wonder if we should choose a more spiritual path to find our greatest good.

The seventh and final cup of the card contains a yellow snake or serpent. Yellow indicates enlightenment once again, and the snake is a symbol for wisdom and infinity. The snake is phallic in nature, indicating that through sexuality and procreation we may find our true purpose.

Debauchery is indicated by this card, in the sense that we can become so overwhelmed by our misperceptions of the energies and pathways being presented to us through these seven cups, that we choose, rather than to balance ourselves through the seven energies of home, wealth, power, courage, intellect, spirituality and sensuousness, just one to focus on.

Overindulgence is the true issue here. Utilizing escapist tendencies and seeking sensatory pleasures in greed, wealth, power, heroism, intellect, spirituality and sensuality are the danger, rather than recognizing the need to have an equitable balance of these gifts of the universe.

In relationship readings, this card indicates that we are not seeing our connection as it truly is. Either we are focused on only the positive, feel good aspects of the union, or we are living in fear of some imagined betrayal. When a relationship is in the early stages of development and this card appears, we can be sure that we are not yet truly in tune with the person we are getting to know.

If we are in an established relationship, this card indicates that we may be unrealistic about the union as it is and that we need to reset the energies between us in order to improve our situation, else we shall continue to live in a false state of being.

The Seven of Cups can also indicate overindulgence in mood altering substances, dependent upon the balance of the spread; a true addiction could be developing.

In other matters, the appearance of the Seven of Cups indicates unrealistic expectations; a sense of fantasy pervades the situation. The man represented in silhouette indicates a lot of subconscious desire and projection taking place that may not be readily apparent at the surface.

The negative tone of this card can be interpreted as one who is living with their head in the clouds and needs to become more grounded in reality.

To divine the intentions of another when this card is active in a spread, one must consider that they have unrealistic fears or expectations of the situation to the point of excess. In timing matters look to seven days or seven weeks for short-term inquiries and the seventh week of Summer for longer-term concerns.

The Eight of Cups

I n our journey into the Suit of Cups thus far we have seen the birth of love, true partnering, celebration, reflection, disappointment, pleasure, nostalgia and illusion. As we move into the energy of the Eight of Cups, we experience Indolence When we move on to the Eight of Cups, we abandon all effort of attaining any of the illusions set forth by the Seven of Cups, we, in a sense, abandon the path we have traveled thus far.

The Eight of Cups symbolizes Indolence. All efforts to achieve goals cease. No energy is expended to further any previous goal. Sloth, laziness and indifference become our attitude as we simply walk away from the situation and people at hand.

Eight cups stand neatly stacked in the forefront as a figure cloaked in red, walking with a staff or wand walks away in the background. The red cloak indicates the passion that was once held for the situation is now diverted in a new direction. The wand that helps him as he pulls away indicates again, that his energy is going in a different direction, away from the cups in the forefront. The figure wears green pants, hoping to gain prosperity of some sort through this abandonment. The landscape itself, even though under moonlight, is green, indicating driving toward new opportunities. The moon is depicted as both the first quarter and the full phases, this indicates that this project will not be returned to, but is considered completed, no more time will be spent here.

When the Eight of Cups appears in a spread you can be sure that an abandonment of some sort is happening. Someone is walking away from the relationship or the situation at hand and is not going to return. It can also mean that someone under the influence of the card is just giving up, feeling that they have exhausted all effort, done the best that they could have and have nothing left to give.

In relationship readings, the Eight of Cups is a time of endings. A decision has been, or will be made, to leave. The subsequent cards in the spread will give you an indication of who or what is being abandoned. If The Eight of Cups falls as an outcome card you need to begin to accept that there will be no further effort put into the relationship on the part of the person you are inquiring about.

In other matters, this card again indicates a change of path, a change of direction, a change of priorities. The previous goals and projects will no longer receive attention.

In a positive tone the Eight of Cups reminds us that new experiences are just ahead of us and if we learn from our past, we may find the people and situations in our future that are better suited to our lifestyles. Learning when to let go is an important lesson in life. We cannot truly move forward unless we release the past.

The negative vibration of this card can lead to depression and anxiety if we feel that we have been abandoned. Again, we must learn to let go and accept the things that we cannot change. The only thing that we can control is ourselves.

To divine the intentions of another when this card appears you can be sure that they are going to turn away from the person or situation at hand.

In timing matters look to eight days to eight weeks for a decision to be reached, for long-term considerations the timing will occur during the eighth week of Summer.

The Nine of Cups

After experiencing the sense of abandonment that can occur as we continue our journey into the Suit of Cups, we, if we have learned our lessons well, can be gifted with the energy of the Nine of Cups, Happiness!

The Nine of Cups brings us the pure and irrevocable energy of being Happy. We feel that all is well in our world and that we can finally enjoy our life. We appreciate the bounty that has come our way and feel very fortunate indeed.

Nine Cups appear neatly arranged as if in anticipation of guests arriving. They sit atop a blue coverlet, blue bringing the purity of the energy of happiness to our attention. The innkeeper is amidst his environment well prepared for the event about to commence. His feet are firmly planted on the floor, his arms are relaxed in a contented pose across his chest, his blue and white robe, indicating purity, does not fully cover his red stockings, referring to his underlying passions, along with his red cap. He wears a contented smile, not only his mouth, but his eyes are smiling with glee as well. The heavy yellow distribution throughout the card represents enlightenment, an opening to sharing this enlightenment with others, as he shares his happiness.

When the Nine of Cups appears in a spread you can be sure that something positive is about to happen. This card has often been interpreted as the "Wish Card", and so it can indicate that whatever the Querent has been hoping or wishing for is about to come true, with good results.

In relationship readings, the Nine of Cups indicates a time of great joy and harmony. Happiness is shared between you and your significant other as well as with your social circle. It often appears when relationships are developing to the next level, perhaps agreeing to an initial commitment of becoming exclusive for those who have been dating casually, or an engagement occurring for those who are more seriously involved, or the purchase of a first home for a couple who is already committed to each other. Good things happen when the Nine of Cups appears in a spread.

In other matters, this card again indicates goals being achieved, results being attained to the Querent's satisfaction and delight.

The negative vibrations of this card are only that this Happiness can be short-lived if the Querent does not remain on the same path of action to ensure that the influence of this card is not fleeting. We must not cease to put effort into cultivating our good fortune when this card is active.

To divine the intentions of another when this card appears you can be sure that they are going to choose a course of action that is well suited to our intentions.

In timing matters, look to nine days to nine weeks for a decision to be reached, for long-term considerations the timing will occur during the ninth week of Summer.

The Ten of Cups

We experienced great joy in the last card of the Suit of Cups, and now we move into the Ten of Cups, which brings us under the influence of Satiety. This is not a fleeting or excited state of satisfaction and happiness, but a more permanent state of being. We have a sense of stability and security.

The Ten of Cups symbolizes Satiety. We have journeyed through the suit of cups and we have finally found gratification. We have learned the lessons of love, coupling, celebration, reevaluation, disappointment, pleasure, illusion, indolence, happiness and we are now blessed with the reward of Satiety.

Satiety is truly a sense of contentment and gratitude. We now understand what it is to love. We now respect that sense of love in ourselves and others. We respect the feelings of others and we know that we honor ourselves as well. We are gracious and benevolent to those less fortunate than ourselves and we enjoy a general state of well-being.

Ten cups arc in the sky on what appears to be a rainbow, representing the energies of passion, enlightenment, purity, prosperity and love. A family appears beneath. The man and woman pose together in a loving embrace, each free hand reaching toward the sky, palm open, gratefully receiving the blessings bestowed. Their two children dance in joy alongside them. The colors of the garments worn by all figures in the picture represent all the energies they have been gifted with that appear above them in the sky.

When the Ten of Cups appears in a spread, we are happy, we are grateful and we are satisfied. We feel safe and happy and we feel that all of our needs have been met. More than anything else, we are thankful for the journey that brought us to this level of contentment; we look forward to further establishing our families and enjoying time with those we love.

In relationship readings, the Ten of Cups indicates a time of blissful commitment and contentment. If our relationships have gone through a difficult phase, we can be sure that the issues are resolved and we are moving forward into a stable and secure progression of our lives together. The Ten of Cups also can indicate the establishment of a home and family, either a traditional family or a nontraditional assembly of family, but family just the same.

In other matters, this card again indicates happiness, security, success and completion. This is one of the most positive cards in the deck and we are well served to offer our gratitude to the powers that guide and influence us.

The negative vibration of this card can occur when we do not give thanks for the blessings and harmonies bestowed upon us and we neglect our relationships, take them for granted, and we may cause them to cycle once again through the lower energies of the Suit of Cups.

To divine the intentions of another when this card appears you can be sure that they are going to bring you a result that makes you feel happy and grateful. Understanding and contentment serve to harmonize our emotions with each other and our commitments are made.

In timing matters, look to ten days to ten weeks for a decision to be reached, for long-term considerations the timing will occur during the tenth week of Summer.

The Page of Cups

The Page of Cups has enjoyed the satisfaction of the Ten, has expressed his gratitude for the blessings bestowed upon him, and he has found a new depth of emotion after the lessons of the Pips. He is just reaching maturity as it pertains to human emotion and the element of water. He has a new level of understanding and an ability to feel on a deeper level than he has before. The Page vibrates to the influence of Pisces, he is beginning to trust his intuition and he is very creative.

The Page is eager to experience love and partnership and offers his heart innocently to the object of his affections. He is sensitive to the feelings of others, he truly cares, and in so being, he is vulnerable. The Page of Cups is the earthy part of water, grounded and sensitive.

The Page, as are all court cards in the suit of water, is dressed in the colors of enlightenment and purity. The spirituality associated with the suit of water is represented in the flowers that adorn his tunic, opening skyward to ever remind us to give thanks. The cup he holds in his right hand contains a fish, a Christian symbol referring to the anglers, Jesus and his apostles, who built a belief system based on kindness and acceptance. One wonders in a more mundane way if the Page is considering releasing the fish into the waters that run behind him, thus setting the fish free and bestowing the ultimate gift upon the creature. He seems to be enjoying his communion with the fish that peaks out of the cup, perhaps the fish is helping him to further establish his intuition through the lessons learned by way of the pip cards.

The Page is eager to experience emotion; he is ready for love and desires that his offers of affection be accepted at face value. The Page is sensitive to the feelings of others and truly does care.

The influence of this card in a relationship reading can indicate that the couple is ready to express honest feelings of love and affection to each other. A loving energy exists between the pair.

In other matters, the card can indicate the need for love and bonding, an appreciation of sincerity, and perhaps the need to refresh a situation that has been stagnant. This Page can bring good news concerning love affairs, births and matters of the heart.

The negative tone of this card can indicate oversensitivity within an individual, wearing one's heart on their sleeve. One being influenced in a negative way by this card will not actively seek love but will only fantasize about it and pine.

To divine the intentions of another when this card appears, consider that they will be very sincere and honest with you and wish to be of emotional support to you in some capacity in your life. A need for bonding will exist in conjunction with shared experiences that can last a lifetime.

In timing matters, the Page of Cups will indicate the eleventh week of Summer for long-term concerns and will translate to either eleven days or eleven weeks for shorter-term matters. This card can also indicate timing occurring during the time that the Sun transits Pisces.

Contrary to popular interpretation, the Page of Cups is unlikely to represent a youthful individual with fair skin and brown or blonde hair. If the physical interpretations of the Tarot were to hold true to the depictions in the artwork on the cards, all physical descriptions would be limited to members of the Caucasian race. To truly understand the card, look to the personality and energies of the card for a description of the individual; do not try to describe physical attributes. Many traditional readers do not expand their interpretations beyond the physical.

Court cards appearing in spreads do not necessarily represent people; they may well be solely representative of the energy in a situation and not a person.

The Knight of Cups

The Knight of Cups comes forward into a relationship offering his cup of love and emotion to his intended, with all the sincerity of emotion expected of the suit of water. He represents the fiery part of water, steamy, with passion and intensity of emotion being his style. Scorpio rules the Knight of Cups, and as with all knights, he is a messenger. This messenger brings news of relationships and family matters.

The Knight predominantly wears the colors of the suit of water, white and blue, as do all court cards of the suit. Fish, red in color, adorn his tunic. Red is indicative of his passionate nature, and the fish representing his spirituality, his emotional core. Blue plumage at the top of his helmet indicates again, purity and his sensitive nature. His horse exudes the energy of the suit, graceful, calm, caring, and stoic; a sense of a calming approach is the energy of this card.

As the horse and rider are facing to the right, this card can indicate a positive movement forward, as when a lover wants to advance a relationship to the next level, whatever that level may be.

In relationships, the Knight of Cups pursues his interest calmly, affectionately and sincerely. He insinuates himself slowly and gently into the life of the intended, and he is not the type to leave in haste. If he feels the relationship crumbling, he will try to work things out before making a final exit.

In relationship readings, the Knight of Cups can indicate a sincere offering of affection and attention; he will also indicate an individual that will romantically pursue your affections. He will be patient in waiting for you to accept his offers of love, but he will not wait forever. The energy of this card can also indicate an individual who is returning to a lover after an absence, or he may be offering a proposal of some sort.

In other matters, look for the energies of passion, intensity and quiet strength. Any period of emotional detachment passes quickly and is eliminated under this Knight's influence.

The negative connotation of this card is one of being overemotional and irrational. Use logic in conjunction with feelings.

To divine the intentions of another when this card is present, you can be sure that they wish to be fair and consider all aspects of your situation. The energy of this card indicates that they will likely make a compromise or counter offer. Individuals under the influence of this card will be willing to negotiate and hold up their end of any agreement made.

In matters of timing look to the twelfth week of Summer and for shorter-term concerns look to twelve days or twelve weeks. This card can also indicate timing occurring during the time that the Sun transits Scorpio.

Contrary to popular interpretation, the Knight of Cups is unlikely to represent a fair-skinned young man with brown or blonde hair. If the physical interpretations of the Tarot were to hold true to the depictions in the artwork on the cards, all physical descriptions would be limited to members of the Caucasian race. To truly understand the card, look to the personality and energies of the card for a description of the individual; do not try to describe physical attributes. Many traditional readers do not expand their interpretations beyond the physical.

Court cards appearing in spreads do not necessarily represent people; they may well be solely representative of the energy in a situation and not a person.

The Queen of Cups

QUEEN of CUPS.

She enjoys being feminine. She wants to nurture and care for all who approach her. She is earthy, motherly, and symbolic of feminine committed love. She is ruled by the sensuous and emotional nature of Scorpio. She enjoys the attraction that men have for her.

She is the watery part of water, fluid and flowing, receptive and passive in nature, but strong-willed just the same. She is possessive and intense concerning those she cares for. She is a good wife and mother and takes true joy in nurturing those around her.

She sits upon her throne, surrounded by the water, which is the element that rules her. At her feet are pebbles washed ashore, treasures from deep within the psyche represented by the water at her feet. She is the keeper of secrets, a woman you can confide in, but she keeps her own counsel. Her throne is adorned with mermaid-like cherubs, indicative of the spirituality and intuition associated with the water she holds dear. Water is representative of the subconscious, those thoughts that we harbor inside and sometimes are unaware of ourselves.

The Queen of Cups is dressed in the colors associated with the energies of her element, water. Blue and white are predominant symbolizing purity, and a yellow crown rests upon her head indicating enlightenment. She holds before her a cup that is reminiscent of the holy grail, a chalice of gold with angels perched to guard the contents, within are the answers to spiritual mysteries thousands of years old. She holds the cup with respect and intends to take good care of the vessel while she holds the throne.

She has a balanced temperament and a desire to nurture than cannot be repressed. She draws men to her by her watery sensuality and chooses the suitor who will best allow her to preside in feminine power over her domain.

In relationship readings, this Queen will indicate a watery female who will be generous and kind with her loved ones. She is a woman who is maternal and caring in nature. Some may find her watery affections quite smothering at times, but others will find these traits endearing.

In other matters, the influence of this Queen will reflect an individual with this type of nature within the focus of the query, or this energy manifesting within the Querent them self.

The negative tone of this card is the maternal nature that can result in an oppressive or codependent need for attention and affection, constantly feeling driven to do more for others than others may wish to have done.

To divine the intentions of another when this card appears in a spread, be aware that the person you are inquiring about will behave in a totally nurturing and giving manor, however, the generosity does not come without a price. The recipient will be expected to be reciprocal in their devotion.

In matters of timing look to the thirteenth week of Summer for long-term concerns and the thirteenth day or week for shorter term concerns. This card can also indicate timing occurring during the time that the Sun transits Scorpio.

Contrary to popular interpretation, the Queen of Cups is unlikely to represent a woman with blonde hair. If the physical interpretations of the Tarot were to hold true to the depictions in the artwork on the cards, all physical descriptions would be limited to members of the Caucasian race. To truly understand the card, look to the personality and energies of the card for a description of the individual; do not try to describe physical attributes. Many traditional readers do not expand their interpretations beyond the physical.

Court cards appearing in spreads do not necessarily represent people; they may well be solely representative of the energy in a situation and not a person.

The King of Cups

The King of Cups is Cancer personified. He is the emotional, nurturing, and loving male, secure in his own emotive actions. The King of Cups is the King of the element of water and rules with sympathy and caring. He considers the feelings of others and is aware of and comfortable with, his emotional and intuitive side.

He represents the airy part of water, that which can be like a fog, or a mist. Intellectual understanding coupled with emotion. This King possesses an innate understanding of the psychological and emotional implications that drive human behavior.

Again, as in all the court cards of the Suit of Cups, we see the King adorned in the colors of purity and enlightenment, yellow and blue. The King also bears a red sash indicating his passion for his spirituality. The golden necklace around his neck bears the symbol of the fish, once again representing the ruling element of water. He holds his golden scepter in his left hand and his cup in his right, showing a balance between action and feeling. This King feels his way through decisions, rather than thinking them over.

His throne floats upon the waters, seemingly disconnected from all land. Water is the element that this King rules. He sees this as his domain and rides atop it. His rule will determine whether the waters are in an uproar, or continue to be serene and smooth.

The King casts his glance to the side, indicating that he is always vigilant over what he perceives to be under his rule.

This King enjoys nurturing projects and enterprises along. He takes pride in seeing the people he is involved with make progress.

In relationship readings, he will generally represent a man who is commitment minded. If a marriage ends, he will actively seek out another committed relationship and remain supportive of his original family as well. This is a man who wishes to give and receive love and has the ability to make those who partner with him feel cared for.

This King will be loyal and faithful to anyone that he loves. If he falls out of love, he will tend to end a relationship to free himself and his partner to find love again. This King wishes to have a partner to truly share his kingdom with, but in order to do so; he must feel loved and appreciated.

This man does require nurturing on a regular basis; he needs to feel appreciated in order to remain strong.

When this card appears in spreads relating to other matters, you are looking at an intuitive and caring energy of management being present, and you will be expected to oversee your responsibilities with great care and concern.

The negative tone of this card is a leaning toward escapism and fantasy from one who is mature enough to know better.

To divine the intentions of others when this card appears, be assured that you will gain the emotional and psychological support of those in a position of authority, but you will be expected to carry out your actions independently.

Contrary to popular interpretation, the King of Cups is unlikely to represent a man with blonde hair. If the physical interpretations of the Tarot were to hold true to the depictions in the artwork on the cards, all physical descriptions would be limited to members of the Caucasian race. To truly understand the card, look to the personality and energies of the card for a description of the individual; do not try to describe physical attributes. Many traditional readers do not expand their interpretations beyond the physical.

Court cards appearing in spreads do not necessarily represent people; they may well be solely representative of the energy in a situation and not a person.

Chapter

5

The Swords

Uncloaking the Tarot:

Understanding and Working Through the Suit of Swords

The Primary Influences of The Swords

The Suit of Swords is representative of the autumn, of things perhaps coming to an end. Many of the pip cards in the Sword suit are associated with pain, or painful forced change, but not all. Swords represent the east quarter of the circle, the element of air, the letter E, and Dawn. Swords represent the intellectual in many cases. (Aquarius, Gemini and Libra).

When Swords are predominant in a spread, expect change and intellectual growth to be occurring in the life of the querent. Intellectual concerns are of primary importance and the Querent may find knowledge, deeper understanding and forced change, for better or worse, occurring in some area of their life.

The Swords are ruled by the element of air, and so are thus associated with the air signs of astrology, Aquarius, Gemini and Libra, as stated above. When the court cards appear they refer to individuals who have strong characteristics of these signs predominant in their personalities, or they may represent the influence of the element of air on the Querent themselves.

The Swords are an intellectual suit; they speak of knowledge, communication, balance and the preparation for and adaptation to change. The Swords are a masculine and unemotional suit, seeking to teach the Querent the lessons of gaining greater understanding of the self and others on a higher level. They have the "unpredictability" of Aquarius, the "mercurial intellect" of Gemini, and the desire for "justice" and balance of Libra.

Negative connotations of the Suit of Swords include loss, grief, stagnation, and cold and callous behavior.

Positive influences of the Suit of Swords include growth, intellectual superiority, understanding, adaptation to change, and quick thinking.

The Swords are associated with the season of autumn. When interpreted symbolically they refer to the autumn of life, humanitarianism, change, and intellectual growth. When asking literal questions concerning timing, look to the autumn months. When referring to a time of day, look to dawn, when all is refreshed and begins anew.

The Swords are the dawn of the Minor Arcana; they bring us to an awakening of a deeper understanding of humankind and an ability to face the changes and challenges that life brings to us all. Change and new beginnings abound when the Swords are about. The Swords are a stern and instructional suit, forcing us through life's lessons. When their influences are applied in a positive light, we grow as individuals and rise to the challenges we are confronted with, but they can cause grief, anguish, and pain, and an inability to cope with loss and change when they vibrate negatively.

Always caution the Querent as to the negative vibration in a spread as well as enlightening them to the positive, as all cards are polar in nature and can have influence in either direction. No one card is purely positive nor purely negative, all seventy-eight cards possess both attributes, focus on the enlightened interpretation of the cards, but always caution as to the negative influences as well.

The Ace of Swords

The Ace of Swords symbolizes piercing through the subconscious into the intellectual knowledge and information of our universe. The Sword can also cut people and things out of our lives with swift and furious force leaving us reeling with the onslaught of enforced change.

All Aces are gifts from God. The artwork shows the "Hand of God" presenting the ability to think with clarity to us. We have no distractions on the landscape in the distance, we are focused as we continue our journey, the gift of this Ace is the ability to discern what we need to release and remove from our lives in order to move forward in a more positive energy.

In relationship readings, the Ace of Swords will indicate the ability to view the relationship realistically and make informed and intelligent decisions concerning the future. It is the intellectual side of a relationship, the sword pictured above being a symbol of cutting to the heart of an issue through intellect. Clarity of thought exits when this card appears in a relationship spread. It can indicate a swift and sudden severing of a tie. The card can also represent new ideas and thought processes to resolve any relationship issues, look to subsequent cards to interpret which way the intellect is likely to decide.

In readings concerning other subject matter it denotes new beginnings, new ideas, we see things much more clearly and feel confident about making decisions at this time. We cut through illusion and begin to see life with more wisdom and acute perception with the Ace of Swords.

The negative intonations of the card, or cautions, can include a swift and total severance of a relationship or a situation with no room for negotiation, a final and decisive action.

When querying another's intentions in a given situation the Ace of Swords indicates that the individual is going to make a decision very soon, within a brief period of time.

When asking about a time frame for an event, the card indicates the first week of Autumn in a long-term estimation, or for reading more immediate concerns it can indicate one day or one week, dependent upon the position in the spread.

The Two of Swords

The Two of Swords takes pause and seeks to balance and justify any forthcoming decision. It is a quiet and contemplative card, as with all twos, seeking balance. It can symbolize a quiet meditative time, a withdrawal from the mainstream to seek answers on the inside.

A figure sits alone at the water edge, blindfolded so as to avoid distraction, hands crossed over the chest whilst balancing two swords and weighing the two paths that are to be chosen from. This minor arcana card is very similar to the major arcana card of Justice, but without the consequences being as far-reaching. The decision being made is more personal in nature. The waning quarter moon in the background indicates that this is a decision that will either end a situation or take it in a new direction.

The figure is dressed in white for purity and yellow shoes indicate a foundation in enlightenment, or new knowledge, being part of the contemplation. A desire to do what is right is represented by the white robe of purity.

Here is a Sword that demonstrates deep thought, as the next step on the journey is carefully considered.

The Two of Swords represents Peace, an inner tranquility that occurs when one knows one has to review and reflect upon a situation, prior to moving forward any further.

In relationship matters, the card represents withdrawal from and quiet contemplation of the affair, before moving forward with any decision or disposition of the relationship.

In other matters, the card expresses temporary, self-imposed isolation, but a welcome break from day-to-day conflict.

The negative tone of this card, or caution, suggests an inability to act and to pause too long while pondering the course of action required, creating an energy of stagnation.

To divine the intentions of another, this card indicates that the person is still considering the situation, and subsequent cards will indicate the most likely outcome of that consideration.

In timing matters, the Two of Swords would indicate the second week of Autumn for a long-term question, for short-range inquiries the approximate timeframe would be two days or two weeks.

The Three of Swords

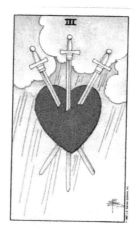

The Three of Swords moves into the painful influence of Sorrow. The path of the Swords is becoming more difficult to traverse. The sadness allows the Querent to grieve that which has been lost.

Three swords pierce a red heart, against a background of dark clouds and rain. The rain represents the tears of sorrow. The red heart indicates something, which we truly care about that, has now changed in a permanent way. The three swords piercing through the heart can also be indicative a three-way love affair, and the Querent may be represented by any one of those three swords. Someone has a sense of love for two separate individuals and may have difficulty deciding which relationship to keep and which relationship to let go, perhaps indefinitely putting off making a decision.

When interpreting this card in a divinatory spread one must always keep in mind the intellectual energy of the Swords and remember that the core influence of this card is one of Sorrow. This means that, whatever the situation at hand may be, someone is going to feel pain; it is inevitable when this energy is present. It is a painful card for all involved.

In relationship readings, this card can indicate a love triangle, a betrayal, or the interference of a third party in the relationship.

In other matters, the card indicates that a choice must be made between two mitigating circumstances. Someone, even the Querent themselves, is going to experience pain regardless of which path is decided upon.

The negative tone of this card is that a painful indecisiveness can prolong periods of stagnation, delay and sorrow. No matter which path is chosen, pain is unavoidable, the only way out is through the pain one wishes to avoid or delay. When this card is active in a spread it is best to consider all options and to be certain of the course of action decided upon, as the pain can be so deep that one causes to another, or to oneself, that a permanent closure to the path not taken is likely to occur.

To divine the intentions of another, keep in mind that again, this card denotes Sorrow, so the person one is inquiring about may well make a decision that will bring you pain and discomfort.

In timing matters, this card denotes the third week of Autumn for long-term matters and indicates an approximate three day or three week period for questions pertaining to more short-term concerns.

The Four of Swords

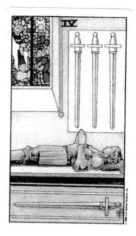

The Four of Swords appearing in a spread is representative of a time of Truce. The betrayal, pain, and sorrow of the three have led one to the four, where isolation and reflection begin the healing process.

Three Swords hover above what appears to be a sarcophagus, with one Sword beneath, at the ready, within arm's length. The sarcophagus is yellow, indicating enlightenment, the Swords representative of the intellect, the thoughts that are on the mind of the one represented by the three swords, being held in consideration, and the sword beneath is that which one already knows. The stained glass window in the background is representative of kindness and generosity, a place of tranquility that the Querent may wish to attain.

The one word to be associated with this card is the word "Truce". This is a quiet and contemplative card, not a card of action, but a card of rest and repose.

In relationship matters, this card indicates that someone is quietly focusing on a relationship and preparing them self for the next interaction. This is not a card of initiation, or taking action, or communicating, but a card of preparing. One will be gathering their thoughts together and planning how to present them when influenced by this card. It is best not to disturb a person under the influence of this energy, but allow them to complete their thought process in peace.

In other matters, this card denotes a sense of withdrawal and thoughtfulness. Goals are being considered and a plan of action is under development

This card can also denote an illness requiring rest in order to recover.

The negative influence of this card can be one in where the Querent becomes stagnant and inactive by allowing oneself to stay in the mode of reflection and contemplation rather than moving forward and determining a course of action.

To divine the intentions of another this cards indicates that the individual in question is feeling a need to think things over without distractions.

In timing matters, this card will indicate the fourth week of Autumn for long-term inquiries and for shorter-term questions, it will indicate an approximated period of four days or four weeks.

The Five of Swords

The Five of Swords makes us feel a sense of Defeat. We have fought our battle, but it seems as though nothing has been won, and nothing has been lost. We have engaged in a futile and fruitless fight.

In the foreground, a figure holds three of the five swords, indicating that he is victorious. The other two figures have laid down their weapons and are making a slow retreat in the background, looking despondent over having left the battlefield. The figure in the forefront is dressed in the colors of red and green, indicating passion and prosperity, yellow boots and hair, indicate an enlightened energy, but yet, he has failed to convince his opponents to join his ranks. A sense of confusion emanates from the figure in the foreground, as he may well know and understand that he is correct and has won his battle, yet his opponents are unconvinced and abandoning the fight.

A sense of confusion comes over the Querent where this card vibrates. The Querent knows that unrest and dissatisfaction exist, yet cannot quite determine exactly what the problem is.

In relationship matters, this card can indicate the inability to reach an agreement, whether it is on level of commitment or decisions concerning the future of the couple. The parties involved will "agree to disagree" and no compromise is achieved. Issues will remain unresolved and further discussion or arguing is useless.

In other matters, negotiations come to a halt and no agreement can be reached. A sense of having achieved a shallow and empty victory may prevail, hence the feeling of Defeat no matter what the outcome of the struggle may be. No resolution to the conflict at hand has yet been found and the Querent feels as if they are in a no-win situation.

The positive influence of this initially negative card can be the ability to recognize a situation that must be left alone. No further expenditure of energy will convince or cajole a change.

To divine the intentions of another when this card appears one must be aware of a sense of resistance within the individual. An uncooperative attitude will exist and further pressing of a matter may cause another to absent themselves from the situation altogether.

In timing matters, look to the fifth week of Autumn for long-term inquiries and for shorter-term concerns this card indicates either five days or five weeks.

The Six of Swords

When the Six of Swords appears in a spread we finally experience some relief from the pain and anxiety of the suit. We can be sure that a passage to smoother waters is apparent in our lives, and a calming effect will begin to overtake our psyches.

The card depicts a man, woman and child making their way from choppy water to the smooth water that allows them to make way to the distant shore. The sky is clear, indicating that emotions are calm. The clothing of the figures is dominated by the color yellow, which represents enlightenment. They are moving forward together with a new understanding of each other due to the suffering they have endured thus far through the pips of the suit of swords. They head toward the horizon, with a cooperative and inclusive attitude, to begin anew.

Science is the one energy of this card, in the sense that through observation, experimentation and the experience we have noted we now understand that we can leave isolation, sorrow and confusion behind. We have learned much thus far in our difficult journey through the suit of Swords and we intend to take those experiences forward with us and apply them to future situations to ensure our success.

In relationship matters this card indicates an end to conflict and the moving into the future together, not alone, having resolved the conflicts with our significant other.

In other matters expect that the Querent will have experienced enough growth to move forward once again with confidence and strength in knowing that things will surely improve.

The negative tone of this card can be a repetitive tendency of trying to start fresh. An inability to learn from past mistakes and thus failing to move to the smoother waters that the card promises, and making the same mistakes over and over again.

In matters of timing this card will indicate the sixth week of Autumn for long-term concerns, for short-term inquiries this card indicates either six days or six weeks.

The Seven of Swords

The Seven of Swords vibrates to a sense of Deception. When this card becomes active in a spread, someone is deceiving the Querent, or the Querent is deceiving someone. The deception could be taking place because the deceiver is afraid that knowledge of the situation will not be met with a sense of understanding, so the Querent should try to understand the reasons for the deception and not focus on the deception itself.

A figure carries away five swords on tiptoe, giving the impression of stealth and caution. The swords do not belong to him. They have been left outside of the carnival in the background, in a sense, people who are leaving their worries behind. The thief is carrying away the swords, symbolically carrying out a deception while we are trying to take our focus away from our worries. We have let our guard down and someone is taking advantage of our lack of vigilance.

The thief wears red boots for passion, blue leggings for purity, a yellow robe of enlightenment and a red cap, again denoting passion. His expression is one of frivolity. He may be taking your ideas and intending to present them as his own, he leaves two swords behind, picking and choosing what he wants and needs in order to advance his own intentions. You may be unaware that a deception is happening at all, as the smiling face of the thief tries to make away with that which is not his.

Deception is an energy to which we all have differing reactions. Some among us become enraged at the thought of being deceived, but we must learn to look at the reasoning behind the deception. Does the thief have such low self esteem that they are afraid to come forward in honesty and ask for what they need? Are they afraid that we will reject them if they allow the façade they present to us to fall away? Before reacting to a deception, try to understand the reasoning behind it and thus make way to clear your relationships of deceptions in the future.

In relationship readings, this card suggests that there is dishonesty between the partners. This card does not necessarily denote infidelity, although it can, but it usually pertains to dishonesty or secretiveness. Many deceptions occur because partners have a fear of jeopardizing the relationship, so compassion and forgiveness should be the initial consideration of the Querent when this card appears.

In other matters, this card refers to stiff competitors or rivals behaving in a dishonest manner. It can also indicate the actual occurrence of an outright theft.

The positive intonation of this card can indicate a sincere attempt by someone to spare another's feelings through hiding the truth from them.

To divine the intentions of another when this card is present you must consider that they will have a hidden agenda geared toward achieving their own goals. Caution should be exercised in order to prevent any unforeseen loss.

In timing matters, this card will indicate the seventh week of Autumn for long-term concerns and it will indicate either seven days or seven weeks for shorter-term concerns.

The Eight of Swords

The Eight of Swords moves us forward through the painful lessons of the Swords into a sense of Isolation. There is an enforced separation and loss of contact when this card becomes active in a spread. An interruption to the flow has occurred and one must again seek solace on one's own on the lonely path of the Sword.

Eight Swords surround a woman who is blindfolded and bound. The Swords represent a prison of sorts. She is blindfolded, so she does not know that she can step forward through the gap that appears in the makeshift bars formed by the swords. A white cloth, which if she only resisted against the wrapping, she could break free of, loosely binds her but yet, she remains still. The Eight Swords surrounding her are her own negative thoughts, she is blind to any outside input.

The Isolation of this card is all about boundaries. She will not step outside her own thoughts nor will she be receptive to outside input. When this card is active in a person's energy, you must just leave that person alone and respect their boundaries until they are ready to remove the restrictions they have set.

If you are the one under the influence of this card, it is wise to open yourself up to outside input and break out of your self-imposed isolation.

In relationship readings there is an inability to affect the situation at hand, one is bound and isolated from the object of one's desires

In other matters, the card represents being shut off and barred from affecting change to the situation at hand.

The positive intonation of this card is the introspection that can bring about wise decision making when this vibration occurs.

To divine the intentions of another when this card is present you can be sure that they are distancing themselves from the issue at hand. Walls are being put up by the individual that will prevent any changes from occurring any time soon.

In timing matters, this card indicates the eighth week of Autumn for long-term concerns and for short-term matters look to eight days or eight weeks.

The Nine of Swords

The Nine of Swords is a nightmarish card that reflects the effects of Cruelty upon the Querent. Anguish and pain haunt the Querent and there does not seem to be a way to defeat the anxiety that plagues us when this card is active in a spread.

A figure weeps alone in bed at night, the card is black, and not even the moon spreads any light near the figure. Nine Swords hover above the figure indicating an inability to shut the worry and negative thoughts off in order to rest. Insomnia is highly probably when this card is active in a person's energy.

The figure finds no comfort in the blanket that adorns the bed, made with fabric of green, yellow and red, for the energies of prosperity, enlightenment and passion. All of the signs of the zodiac appear on the bedspread; indicating that in due course, time will alleviate the suffering. If the figure could only open his eyes to the warmth and comfort afforded by the quilt on the bed, some peace and comfort from the Cruelty of the world could be found, but the figure is too focused on their pain and anxiety to recognize the comfort that is readily available.

In relationship readings, we may feel hurt, worried, anxious and abandoned. We cannot see how things will ever improve and we continue to feed our own fears making our distressed condition worse. Perhaps our worst fears are confirmed, we must face the harsh and cruel situation not only during the night when sleep eludes us, but also in the cold light of day that ensues.

In other matters, we have been dealt a blow that is painful and can in fact, be devastating. Strength is required when this card is active in our energy as we are being confronted with a difficult situation on our journey. We must escape into our intellect and refuse to let the painful emotions associated with this card overrule our psyche.

The positive tone of this card can be that now that we have had our worst fears realized, we can let go and move forward. We are stronger for having suffered this Cruelty and our characters are developing a sense of humility and compassion as we have a true understanding of pain.

To divine the intentions of another in reference to the energy of this card you can be sure that they are suffering under the weight of a decision that they know will bring pain to those involved.

In timing matters, look to the ninth week of Autumn for long-term issues and for short term concerns look to nine days or nine weeks.

The Ten of Swords

The culmination of grief and loss occurs when the Ten of Swords appears in a spread. This is one of the most difficult cards in the deck to deal with. Ruin is the sense associated with this card, betrayal, a sense of being stabbed in the back, yet knowledge that one can rise up once more and face the anguish and emotional loss associated with this card.

A figure lies face down in the sand at the shoreline with ten swords protruding from his back. The sky is black as when we are experiencing the new moon, the absence of the light of the sun reflecting in the night sky. The new moon is a time when we need to cleanse and rid ourselves of negativity; it denotes the ending of a cycle, as does the Ten of Swords.

Although the figure appears to be lifeless, if we look closely we see that his exposed hand forms the mudra for "all is well". We may be down now, but cloaked in passion, purity and enlightenment, represented by the colors of his wardrobe, we will be washed clean by the waters of the ocean and rise again, spiritually and emotionally cleansed. The ten swords are placed in position to clear the chakras and release built up negative energy at all levels, hence the cleansing nature of this ruinous card.

The Ten of Swords completes our journey and lessons of change, loss, gain, and the endless cycle that is both the curse and the blessing of this life. With Ruin comes an ending, and with all endings come new beginnings, the Querent must be advised that a loss always brings us opportunities for new challenges and spiritual, emotional and intellectual growth.

In relationship readings, this card can refer to a very painful ending quite possibly with feelings of betrayal attached to the separation.

In other matters, we find Ruin is the influence that is predominant, and we must prepare ourselves for loss and perhaps a sense of betrayal. Life is infrequently fair and balanced. This is a period when we will feel that many energies are working against us.

In health matters, this card can indicate a need to undergo surgery.

The positive influence of this card is knowing that as one cycle comes to an end, a new and fresh beginning awaits us.

In timing matters, look to the tenth week of Autumn for long-term concerns and for short-term inquiries look to ten days or ten weeks.

The Page of Swords

PAGE of SWORDS.

The Page of Swords has suffered the anguish of the Ten and has found a new courage to face unappealing changes after the lessons of the pips. He is just reaching maturity as it pertains to intellectual growth. The suit of air brings a new level of understanding and an ability to think on a deeper level. The Page vibrates to the influence of the Astrological Sign of Aquarius; he is beginning to trust his experience and he is very analytical. He represents the earthy part of air, using his energy to pursue intellectual pleasures and knowledge.

The Page, as all court cards in the suit of air, is dressed in the colors of enlightenment and passion. His tunic is plain and brown, indicating that he is well grounded. He holds his sword aloft in a way that suggests he is defensive, prepared to battle if necessary over his ideals. The Page of Swords is vigilant and is very aware of his surroundings.

The Page is eager to experience challenge and education and offers his intellect innocently to the world around him. The page is analytical of others feelings and truly understands

The influence of this card in a relationship reading can indicate that there is a level of discomfort or distrust between the couple. One partner is over vigilant and unable to relax within the pairing. An over active state of defensiveness may also exist in one of the partners, caused again, by a lack of trust.

This Page can bring unwanted news in a humanitarian manner.

In other matters, the card can indicate the need for attentiveness, to exercise caution and be sure that one has all of the facts. The Page of Swords can indicate that someone is spying on or literally stalking another in an attempt to analyze their motives.

The negative tone of this card can indicate an immature attitude toward humanity in general and a need and desire to spread gossip.

To divine the intentions of another when this card appears, consider that they will be vigilant with you and your actions. They have not yet come to a point where they truly trust you and may also behave in a defensive manner toward you.

In timing matters, the Page of Swords will indicate the eleventh week of Autumn for long-term concerns and will translate to either eleven days or eleven weeks for shorter-term matters. This card can also indicate timing occurring during the time that the Sun transits Aquarius.

Contrary to popular interpretation, the Page of Swords is unlikely to represent a youthful individual with red or brown hair. If the physical interpretations of the Tarot were to hold true to the depictions in the artwork on the cards, all physical descriptions would be limited to members of the Caucasian race. To truly understand the card, look to the personality and energies of the card for a description of the individual; do not try to describe physical attributes. Many traditional readers do not expand their interpretations beyond the physical.

Court cards appearing in spreads do not necessarily represent people; they may well be solely representative of the energy in a situation and not a person.

The Knight of Swords

KNIGHT of SWORDS .

The Knight of Swords rushes onto the scene impulsively, acting on his first impression of a situation with all the intense mobility that the element of air can muster, like a hurricane or tornado arriving out of nowhere. He is the fiery part of air, fanning the flames of communication into a fury. Aquarius rules the Knight of Swords, and as with all knights, he is a messenger. This messenger brings news of conflicts, anger, discord, troubles and loss.

The Knight wears the colors of the suit of air, silver and red, as do all court cards of the suit. Birds adorn his tunic as they live in and fly through the air above us. His white horse exudes the energy of the suit, swiftness and aggressiveness, a need for haste is the energy of this volatile card. His sword is raised and ready to strike, the energy of hostility can be felt by his posture.

As the horse and rider are facing to the left, this card can indicate a speedy return, as when a lover has been absent and suddenly reappears, however, the return may indicate a confrontation is likely.

In relationships, the Knight of Swords pursues his interest with great analytical adeptness; he assesses a situation and cuts to the heart of the matter at hand with his sharp blade. He is pursuing his intended with the fiery intelligence that ignites his passion; he may be a great speaker or writer when expressing his emotions.

In relationship readings, the Knight of Swords can indicate a swift and sudden return, but also an angry confrontation. He may be gone just as quickly as he arrived if he feels misunderstood or unappreciated. The energy of this card can also indicate an individual who may react hastily in a negative way without knowing all of the facts.

In other matters look for impulsive activity, any period of stagnation passes quickly under the influence of this Knight.

The negative connotation of this card implies a delight in being the bearer of bad news.

To divine the intentions of another when this card is present you can be sure that they do not want to stop to consider all the mitigating factors of your situation, they will react based on their first impressions. The energy of this card indicates that they will likely make a quick decision and perhaps an error in judgment unless supported by more stable cards. Individuals under the influence of this card will behave impulsively and aggressively.

In matters of timing, look to the twelfth week of Autumn and for shorter-term concerns look to twelve days or twelve weeks. This card can also indicate timing occurring during the time that the Sun transits Aquarius.

Contrary to popular interpretation, the Knight of Swords is unlikely to represent a young man with dark hair. If the physical interpretations of the Tarot were to hold true to the depictions in the artwork on the cards, all physical descriptions would be limited to members of the Caucasian race. To truly understand the card, look to the personality and energies of the card for a description of the individual; do not try to describe physical attributes. Many traditional readers do not expand their interpretations beyond the physical.

Court cards appearing in spreads do not necessarily represent people; they may well be solely representative of the energy in a situation and not a person.

The Queen of Swords

She enjoys being independent and intelligent. She wants to educate and enlighten all who approach her. She is airy, aloof, and symbolic of feminine independence. She is ruled by the brilliant and humanitarian nature of Aquarius. She analyzes the attraction men have for her and their motives.

The Queen of Swords is the watery part of air, misty and humid, aggressive and intellectual in nature, but feminine just the same. She is encouraging and protective concerning those she cares for. She is an independent woman whether within the bounds of a committed relationship or not. She encourages her children to experience all that life has to offer and to learn and grow from it.

She sits upon her white throne with angels and butterflies representing the element of air that she rules. She wears a yellow crown of butterflies, indicating intellectual enlightenment. Her blue cloak, the color which relates to purity, is adorned with white clouds, again relating to her element of air. A red necklace and the red veil hanging from the back of her crown and covering her head indicate her passion is of the mind. She holds her sword in her right hand as she welcomes people to approach her, ready to cut through any confusion to the pure facts of the matter in order to provide clear guidance.

She has a calm and aloof nature and is clinical in nearly all of her decision-making. She draws men to her by her airy independence and strength and chooses the suitor who will best appreciate, support and enhance her knowledge of the world.

In relationship readings, this Queen can indicate a career oriented and analytical woman. She can also indicate an upcoming separation as traditionally this card represented women who were divorced or widowed. She is a woman who revels in her superior intellect and draws or repels people through intensity of thought. Of all the Queens, she is the most independent and most comfortable leading a life without a husband.

In other matters, the influence of this Queen will reflect an individual with this type of nature within the focus of the query or this energy manifesting within the Querent them self.

The negative tone of this card indicates the detached and domineering female attributes used to manipulate those around her.

To divine the intentions of another when this card appears in a spread be aware that the person you are inquiring about will behave in a totally independent, intellectual and analytical manner.

In matters of timing look to the thirteenth week of Autumn for long-term concerns and the thirteenth day or week for shorter-term concerns. This card can also indicate timing occurring during the time that the Sun transits Aquarius.

Contrary to popular interpretation, the Queen of Swords is unlikely to represent a woman with dark hair. If the physical interpretations of the Tarot were to hold true to the depictions in the artwork on the cards, all physical descriptions would be limited to members of the Caucasian race. To truly understand the card, look to the personality and energies of the card for a description of the individual; do not try to describe physical attributes. Many traditional readers do not expand their interpretations beyond the physical.

Court cards appearing in spreads do not necessarily represent people; they may well be solely representative of the energy in a situation and not a person.

The King of Swords

The King of Swords is Gemini personified. He is the mercurial, duplicitous, and intellectual male, secure in his own realm of thought. The King of Swords is the King of the element of air. Her rules with unemotional detachment and analytical prowess, he considers the motives of others and is aware of and comfortable with his own analytical side. This King generally represents a man who is single or divorced and may have a career based on intellect rather than physicality.

He represents the airy part of air, that which can be swirls about, around and through each other, perhaps creating thunder from time to time as ideologies clash.

The King of Swords understands the motivational psychology of his subjects and family and does his best to preserve their intellectual growth and mental stability.

Again, as in all the court cards of the Suit of Swords, we see the King adorned in the colors of purity and enlightenment, yellow and blue. The King also bears a purple cloak to indicate his power and authority. The red hood beneath his crown represents his passion for intellect. His golden crown bears the image of an angel, indicating that he rules the heavens above as well as the earthly plane. Butterflies representing the energy of the element of air adorn his throne. His feet rest on a green carpet representing a foundation of prosperity.

The King casts his glance forward, indicating that he is progressive in his thought process as he reaches decisions.

This King enjoys the developmental stages of new enterprises, but then usually hands the ideas over to someone else to work out the details.

In relationship readings, he will generally represent a man who is committed to the woman he loves, yet enjoys meeting and communicating with other women as well. He has a strong need for separateness even within the boundaries of his relationship. He will tend to put the needs of himself before the needs of others if forced to choose.

Although loyal to those he loves, he can continue to be flirtatious throughout his lifetime, as he enjoys the mental stimulation of word play.

This man does require intellectual challenges and stimulation on a regular basis.

When this card appears in spreads relating to other matters you are looking at an intellectualized energy of management being present and you will be expected to follow through with any ideas that you present.

The negative tone of this card is a leaning toward harsh analytics when compassion may be required.

To divine the intentions of others when this card appears be assured that you will gain clarity through the input of those in a position of authority but you will be held accountable for the outcomes of any ideas you implement.

Contrary to popular interpretation, the King of Swords is unlikely to represent a man with dark hair. If the physical interpretations of the Tarot were to hold true to the depictions in the artwork on the cards, all physical descriptions would be limited to members of the Caucasian race. To truly understand the card, look to the personality and energies of the card for a description of the individual; do not try to describe physical attributes. Many traditional readers do not expand their interpretations beyond the physical.

Court cards appearing in spreads do not necessarily represent people; they may well be solely representative of the energy in a situation and not a person.

Chapter

6

The Pentacles

Uncloaking the Tarot:

Understanding and Working Through the Suit of Pentacles

The Primary Influences of The Pentacles

The fourth Suit, Pentacles, represents all that is material, and successes on the earthly plane. Work and family are closely associated with this suit. It is associated with the element of earth, the north quarter of the circle, the season of winter and the time of day of night. Typically, a Pentacle appearing in a spread will indicate stability and security in some manner. The Qabalah assigns the letter A from the ancient Hebraic alphabet to it. (Taurus, Virgo, Capricorn).

When Pentacles are predominant in a spread, expect stability and material growth will be occurring in the life of the Querent. Material and security concerns are of primary importance and the Querent may find career or financial growth, deeper relationships and stabilizing influences, occurring in their life.

The Pentacles are ruled by the element of earth, and so are thus associated with the earth signs of astrology, Taurus, Virgo and Capricorn, as stated above. When the court cards appear they refer to individuals who have strong characteristics of these signs predominant in their personalities, or they may represent the influence of the element of earth on the Querent them self.

The Pentacles are a materialistic and earthy, sometimes sensual suit. They speak of commitment, financial success, home and family, and are a stabilizing force in life. The Pentacles are a feminine and earthy suit, seeking to teach the Querent the lessons of reward, commitment, and achievement in earthly endeavors. They have the taste for luxury of Taurus, the analytical intellect of Virgo, and the sense of commitment and drive toward success of Capricorn.

Negative connotations of the Suit of Pentacles include greed, abandonment, possessiveness, and focus on earthly gain only.

Positive influences of the Suit of Pentacles include emotional growth, industriousness, stability, material growth, and establishing a firm foundation.

The Pentacles are associated with the season of winter. When interpreted symbolically they refer to the winter of life, materialism, career, and material growth. When asking literal questions concerning timing, look to the winter months. When referring to a time of day, look to night, when all is slowed and calmed awaiting a new day.

The Pentacles are the night of the Minor Arcana; they bring us to a peaceful and restful point where we know we have worked hard to achieve what we have. We are allowed to rest and recuperate in the arms of the ones we love, awaiting the next cycle of growth. Prosperity and contentment are active when the Pentacles appear. The Pentacles are a rewarding and favorable suit, blessing us for what we have put our hearts and minds to thus far, giving us repose prior to moving on. When their influences are applied in a positive light, we grow as individuals and rise to our commitments and we prosper, but they can cause us to lose sight of the big picture and unduly focus on our material lives when they vibrate negatively.

Always caution the Querent as to the negative vibration in a spread as well as enlightening them to the positive, as all cards are polar in nature and can have influence in either direction. No one card is purely positive nor purely negative, all seventy-eight cards possess both attributes, focus on the enlightened interpretation of the cards, but always caution as to the negative influences as well.

The Ace of Pentacles

The Ace of Pentacles symbolizes achieving the material rewards that we have strived so long to attain. This card begins the suit which is ruled by the element of earth, denoting stability, prosperity, creativity and commitment. The Ace is a healthy card and can be interpreted in several ways based upon the context of the question at hand.

All Aces are gifts from God. The artwork shows the "Hand of God" presenting the ability to be prosperous, secure and happy to us. We see a beautiful garden before us, which gives one a sense of safety. Outside the archway to the garden, we see a snowy mountain in the distance that seems cold and remote. We can leave the garden if we choose to, much like Adam and Eve in the Garden of Eden, but we do not have to do so, we can stay here and enjoy the blessings the universe has bestowed upon us.

In relationship readings, the Ace of Pentacles will indicate an offering of serious commitment and exclusivity, even to the level of a literal engagement, with the pentacle being offered representing a diamond ring. It is the security side of a relationship, the pentacle pictured above being an offering of all the elements, earth, air, fire, water and spirit. The card can also represent stability in the material sense as well.

Beginnings and new endeavors are born when this Ace becomes active in a spread, we are ready to work hard to achieve our goals and this ace promises that we have stepped onto the correct path.

In readings concerning other subject matters, it denotes offerings, beneficial offerings, such as a new job or salary increase. The card represents the beginning of a new cycle of security and abundance.

The negative intonations of the card, or cautions, can include excessive materialism, greed, clinging to ones' possessions and money too tightly and looking to increase material prosperity through relationships.

When querying another's intentions in a given situation, the Ace of Pentacles indicates that the individual is going to make an offer of a commitment of some sort very soon.

When asking about a time frame for an event the card indicates the first week of Winter in a long-term estimation, or for reading more immediate concerns it can indicate one day or one week, dependent upon the position in the spread.

The Two of Pentacles

The Two of Pentacles takes pause and seeks to balance and justify any forthcoming decision concerning our career, relationship or family. We are trying to pay the proper amount of attention to our responsibilities and maintain a healthy balance between them.

A man stands on one foot and appears to be in a juggling posture with the two pentacles he holds. The pentacles are encircled by a green rope, green representing prosperity, and the rope forming the infinity sign. The figure wears the colors of yellow, for enlightenment, red, for passion and green, again for prosperity. His expression is one of concern as he wants to maintain a balance, he does not wish to drop his pentacles and suffer a loss. Two ships appear on the waves in the background, they may be entering the harbor and the man may need his pentacles to do business with the occupants, or perhaps they are leaving and the man is wondering if he struck the proper bargain or not. The infinity symbol reminds us that there is a larger purpose to life than the mere material side, to keep sight of our spirituality as well as our earthly concerns.

The Two of Pentacles represents Change. We are on the brink of making a change and weighing our options, our costs and benefits, what the effect on our lives will be.

When the Two of Pentacles appears it can indicate a temporary pause, but a Change is likely to occur in the near future.

In relationship matters, the card represents a pause, a time to think things over before taking the relationship to the next level. It also can indicate a struggle for balance within the relationship or a struggle for balance between independence and having a significant other.

In other matters, the card indicates a pause in order to reflect upon the options available and the likely effects of those options. It can also be indicative of an individual who is struggling to maintain a balanced life.

The negative aspect of this card can be a fear of change and thus ensuring our stagnation in our current situation, positive or negative, and allowing ourselves to continue to precariously balance our lives on an ongoing basis.

To divine the intentions of another, this card indicates that the person is still considering the situation, and subsequent cards will indicate the most likely outcome of that consideration.

In timing matters, the Two of Pentacles would indicate the second week of Winter for a long-term question, for short-range inquiries the approximate timeframe would be two days or two weeks.

The Three of Pentacles

The Three of Pentacles appearing at any point in a spread indicates an area in our life where we will apply ourselves and work hard to get ahead. We are like the artisan who has finished his first work and is awaiting payment or recognition. The path of the Pentacles is becoming more prosperous.

The Three of Pentacles brings us to the energy of Work.

A sculptor stands upon a bench, apparently having just completed the archway above. Three Pentacles adorn the archway; the pattern is reminiscent of a celtic knot, representing the endless continuation of beginnings and endings, infinity. There is a spiritual atmosphere to the setting of this card, as it appears that a monk is one of the figures reviewing the design against the artwork produced by the sculptor. The monk representing purity, while the hooded figure, dressed in the colors of passion and enlightenment is indicative of a passion for spirituality.

When interpreting this card in a divinatory spread it can relate to ceremonies of a religious nature, such as baptisms and confirmations. It is also an indicator of receiving recognition for work well done.

In relationship readings, this card can indicate a relationship that has begun, been recognized, and those involved believe that it has the potential to grow into more. It bodes well for the couple involved as it indicates that the match is compatible, each partner recognizes the value of the other.

In other matters, the card advises the Querent to continue moving forward on their chosen path, whether it is in relationship to love, career, spirituality or education. Rewards are just around the corner if one continues to apply them self wholeheartedly.

The negative aspect of this card can be a sense that the level achieved is "good enough", and a tendency to stagnate at the current level, much as the classic "underachiever" would cease to move forward.

To divine the intentions of another, they are highly likely to make decisions in your favor, as they view you as competent and responsible. You will receive the recognition that you deserve.

In timing matters, this card denotes the third week of Winter for long-term matters and indicates an approximate three day or three week period for questions pertaining to more short-term concerns.

The Four of Pentacles

The Four of Pentacles is representative of Possessiveness. The achievements of the three have led one to the four, where we firmly wish to hold on to what we have gained thus far.

A man, giving the impression of wealth and royalty by his attire, sits above a city and clings tightly to the pentacles of the card. His feet are planted firmly on the two pentacles below him, his red boots indicating a passion for material wealth. His arms clutch a pentacle to his chest, indicating a love of the material, and a pentacle rests upon his head, indicating he can think of nothing other than his own prosperity. His back is turned on his kingdom, indicating that he is inattentive to the welfare of others, even those he is responsible for, due to his obsession with wealth.

In relationship matters, the Four of Pentacles indicates that someone is extremely possessive within the context of the relationship, perhaps to the point of obsession. Someone is trying to hold on to the relationship with all their might for fear of losing what they perceive as theirs. This can also indicate a person who chooses a mate based on financial standing, rather than emotional bonding and compatibility.

In other matters, this card denotes a sense of greed. This is a prosperous person who does not wish to share his or her good fortune with anyone. An excessive focus on the material side of life prevents the person from enjoying a healthy balance.

The positive influence of this card can be one in where the Querent becomes committed to a purpose and uses all the power one possesses to achieve one's goals. Supporting cards in the spread will be indicative of success when this card vibrates to the positive.

To divine the intentions of another, this card indicates that the individual in question will behave in a way that is self-serving and not take the wants and needs of others into consideration.

In timing matters, this card will indicate the fourth week of Winter for long-term inquiries and for shorter-term questions, it will indicate an approximated period of four days or four weeks.

The Five of Pentacles

The Five of Pentacles brings the influence of Worry into a spread. We have earned and achieved thus far through the pips of the Pentacles, but we are suffering a setback of some sort. Perhaps while under the influence of the four, we held on so tightly to the material energies we valued so highly, that we lost sight of the importance of balance in our life, and now are paying the price.

Two figures, male and female, are struggling through the snow. Their postures indicate they are cold and suffering. Their clothes, through the colors they bear, are representative of the energies of passion, purity and enlightenment, but they are frayed and in tatters. The male has a cast on his leg and hobbles along on crutches, while the woman walks barefoot in the snow. A sense of loss permeates the card. The stained glass window behind them hosts five pentacles in a shape that is reminiscent of the tree of life, warmth emanates from the beyond the window, as no falling snow is near it. Will the couple find shelter inside? Perhaps an infusion of spirituality will ease their pain, as one gets the sense that the window is contained in a house of worship. An uncertainty brings the energy of Worry into a spread.

A sense of loss comes over the Querent when this card vibrates. The Querent knows that a relationship or a material concern is at risk, and is not quite sure how to protect it at this time. A relationship may be ending, a home may be lost, or a career path disrupted if this card is prominent in a spread. Asking a follow up question as to how one can prevent this loss can provide insight in most cases.

Worry is the one key word to associate with this card when taken at face value.

In relationship matters, this card can indicate a painful ending.

In other matters, worry and fearing an impending loss, can prevent one from moving forward to change the outcome. A sense of humility is required to be released from Worry and perhaps a return to a more spiritual outlook on life will be beneficial.

The positive influence of this troublesome card is a sense of commitment to make it through the bad times together, "for better or worse", and relying on each other to make it to the next cycle.

To divine the intentions of another when this card appears one must be aware that your hopes are not likely to be realized.

In timing matters, look to the fifth week of Winter for long-term inquiries and for shorter-term concerns this card indicates either five days or five weeks.

The Six of Pentacles

When the Six of Pentacles appears in a spread we again experience Success! We can be sure that assistance from a generous friend or employer is arriving, we have found a benefactor that will help to lift us up materially and emotionally after the worry and loss of the five.

In studying the card, we see what appear to be two poor people receiving charity from a prosperous man. The man wears green boots, indicating his foundation in prosperity, a blue and white tunic that indicates his intentions are pure and benevolent, a red cloak and cap represent his passion for helping others in their time of need. He holds the scales of justice in his left hand, he is not to be taken advantage of, but will assist those who truly need his aide.

The card emanates an energy of generosity and kindness.

Success comes to us when we may have been on the verge of abandoning all hope.

In relationship matters, this card can indicate the beginning of sharing our individual resources; a generous atmosphere surrounds the relationship, both partners giving, receiving and sharing. This card can also refer to mutual emotional support between partners.

In other matters, this card can indicate financial increase or reward, such as a raise, a promotion or a recognition of one's abilities on the earthly plain. Financial obligations are met and a feeling of hope for the future is restored.

The negative tone of this card can be a fixation on material gain that leads us to abandon our emotional and spiritual side. The danger is that one may always be seeking a bail out, after having had a fortunate gift from someone in a position to help. It is important to retain a sense of gratitude and to carry the generosity one has received forward to help others in turn.

In matters of timing, this card will indicate the sixth week of Winter for long-term concerns, for short-term inquiries, this card indicates either six days or six weeks.

The Seven of Pentacles

The Seven of Pentacles vibrates to a sense of Frustration. When this card becomes active in a spread, we feel that the seeds we have sown have not born the fruit that we intended to harvest. We feel that we have done everything in our power to tend and care for our garden, but yet the garden stubbornly refuses to yield to our care.

A man stands gazing at a vine that he has been tending, six pentacles remain on the vine, but one pentacle has fallen to the ground, spoiled. His posture is one that suggests disappointment, feeling that his hard work has been wasted; however, he needs to tend to the six remaining pentacles and successfully harvest them, lest they fall to the ground and shrivel as well. His clothing suggests he understands the energies of enlightenment, represented by his yellow boots, purity by his blue leggings and sleeves, and passion represented by his red tunic, but yet he must learn the lesson of patience to divert his energy away from Frustration.

In relationship readings, the significant other not responding or returning the affections of the Querent in a like manner can cause the Frustrastion. One may feel that they are not appreciated or loved enough, and continues to wait for love to blossom.

In other matters, this card refers to limited results, a feeling that the return on your investment is not what you had expected it to be, resulting in Frustration.

The positive influence of this card can be the ability to be patient, wait, and continue to tend to our garden so that it does indeed bear the fruit that sustains our souls.

To divine the intentions of another when this card is present you must consider that they may be wondering what gratification they will receive should they act in support of your desires. They may see a limited benefit and therefore may decide that choosing a path that supports you is not in their best interest or worth their time and energy.

In timing matters, this card will indicate the seventh week of Winter for long-term concerns and it will indicate either seven days or seven weeks for shorter-term concerns.

The Eight of Pentacles

The Eight of Pentacles moves us forward through the Pentacles into a sense of Apprenticeship. We are about to become a student in some area of our life, either a new experience in our work life, or perhaps learning about a new level of commitment and understanding in another area of our life. Be prepared to be taught at this point, as you will not be the journeyman in this situation, but the apprentice.

A man is seated on a workbench chiseling out pentacles, focused on his task. Five pentacles hang above him, recently completed; he is busy working on the sixth and has two more waiting for him to work on. His red leggings and shoes indicate he is passionate about his work, and his blue tunic shows a purity of intention, he wishes to do a good job. He wants to show that he can master the task at hand in order to continue advancing forward through life.

In relationship readings, there is a new viewpoint concerning the relationship, a new understanding of give and take, and a deepening of the sense of commitment, as we learn what it means to truly love one another. A true effort is put forth into cooperating and moving forward in a partnership.

In other matters, this can indicate a change of careers, a return to education, or a change on the educational path. We are entering a learning cycle of life that may be unexpected at this time.

The negative influence of this card can be an inability to learn the lesson being presented and having to repeat the lesson until one successfully comprehends the material that is being presented.

To divine the intentions of another when this card is present, you can be sure that they wish to truly understand any concept that you are presenting. They will study and examine all pertinent information in order to be sure that they are making the correct decisions.

In timing matters, this card indicates the eighth week of Winter for long-term concerns and for short-term matters look to eight days or eight weeks.

The Nine of Pentacles

The Nine of Pentacles vibrates to Abundance. We have learned our earthly lessons and are now allowed to reap what we have sown. Our gardens are healthy and fruitful and we can rejoice at the time of our harvest.

A woman stands in a lush garden wearing a yellow robe, symbolic of enlightenment, adorned with what appear to be red flowers, for passion, but also reminiscent of the astrological symbol for Venus, indicating fertility. A falcon, bearing a red hood, rests upon her gloved hand, the hunt is sure to be successful when she releases him. Her posture is one of relaxation and calm, she has all that she needs in her bountiful surroundings. Six pentacles to her left form the shape of the tree of life, and the three pentacles at her right side form a celtic knot, representing infinity. We are safe in this luscious garden; all of our needs are satisfied.

One is experiencing a rewarding time of life when the Nine of Pentacles is active in a spread. Familial and material concerns are well taken care of and we can relax and enjoy what we have worked so hard to attain.

In relationship readings, a blissful energy of contentment and creativity abounds. We feel secure in our connections and we feel that we are working together to build a solid relationship.

In other matters, we can expect a sense of prosperity. We feel a sense of security and well-being. We feel that we have everything that we need to enjoy life at this point in time.

The negative tone of this card can be a self-centered focus on ourselves and our small worlds, and forgetting to include our societal partners in the celebration of our good fortune.

To divine the intentions of another in reference to the energy of this card you can be sure that any decisions made will please you and bring you fortunate results.

In timing matters, look to the ninth week of Winter for long-term issues and for short-term concerns look to nine days or nine weeks.

The Ten of Pentacles

The culmination of our efforts are achieved when the Ten of Pentacles appears in a spread. Wealth is the keyword in interpreting this card. Prosperity abounds, our home is being established and we can well provide for our loved ones.

Ten Pentacles are in the forefront of the card, six above and four below, reminiscent of the shape of the tree of life. We see three generations of people, an elderly man, seemingly the patriarch of the family rests in the foreground, petting one of the two white dogs. He is dressed colorfully, giving one the impression of a happy occasion. A couple dances in front of him, dressed in the colors that represent passion, purity, and enlightenment. A child reaches out from behind what we can assume is the mother and pets the second dog, giving an overall impression of a family who is enjoying being together under one roof. The room is well decorated which gives you the sense that the family is prosperous and enjoying all that life has to offer.

The Ten of Pentacles completes our journey through the lessons of our work ethic, our commitments to our families and our sense of material well being. With Wealth comes responsibility, we are no longer carefree and responsible only for ourselves, we are established and successful individuals who must tend to our gardens and our families and contribute to our community.

In relationship readings, this card can refer to a couple making a serious commitment to each other and to their futures. It can indicate the establishment of a family and a home. The Ten of Pentacles will indicate that a commitment to each other is being made.

In other matters, we find a sense of security, stability and material gain when this card is active in a spread. We have the love and support of those close to us and we also have the material resources we need to feel fortunate.

The negative influence of this card can be an inability to be charitable and to open our hearts and our homes to those who may need our assistance. When this card vibrates negatively, it can indicate a person who has a fear of, and an inability to make commitments.

In timing matters, look to the tenth week of Winter for long-term concerns and for short-term inquiries look to ten days or ten weeks.

The Page of Pentacles

The Page of Pentacles is ready to embark on a new level of emotional and earthly understanding. He is a blank slate ready to be written upon at a deeper level of comprehension of human nature. He has enjoyed the prosperity and the security of the suit of Pentacles, and now must learn how to give back to the world on the same level at which he has received his blessings. He is ruled by the sign of Capricorn, and he represents the earthy part of earth, using his energy to pursue security of a material and emotional nature.

The Page is dressed in the colors of enlightenment, prosperity and passion. He stands alone in a lush field, gazing at the Pentacle he holds before him as if inquiring as to which direction to take to seek his fortune

The Page is eager to love and establish his career. He offers his earthy nature innocently to the world around him. The Page is sensual and sympathetic to those that encounter him.

The influence of this card in a relationship reading can indicate that the couple is ready to become exclusive and truly investigate whether or not this can be a life-long pairing. A spirit of working together toward common goals exists between the pair when the Page of Pentacles appears in a spread.

This Page can bring welcome news in a celebratory manner.

In other matters, the card can indicate that someone is ambitious and eager to promote them self at work, home, and in society in general.

The negative tone of this card can indicate an immature individual who is lazy, greedy, and looking for an easy way to get ahead, an opportunist. One being influenced in a negative way by this card will manipulate others to their own benefit.

To divine the intentions of another when this card appears, consider that they will be enthusiastic and optimistic about advancing the cause at hand. A sense of support and teamwork will prevail.

In timing matters, the Page of Pentacles will indicate the eleventh week of Winter for long-term concerns and will translate to either eleven days or eleven weeks for shorter-term matters. This card can also indicate timing occurring during the time that the Sun transits Capricorn.

Contrary to popular interpretation, the Page of Pentacles is unlikely to represent a youthful individual with dark hair. If the physical interpretations of the Tarot were to hold true to the depictions in the artwork on the cards, all physical descriptions would be limited to members of the Caucasian race. To truly understand the card, look to the personality and energies of the card for a description of the individual; do not try to describe physical attributes. Many traditional readers do not expand their interpretations beyond the physical.

Court cards appearing in spreads do not necessarily represent people; they may well be solely representative of the energy in a situation and not a person.

The Knight of Pentacles

The Knight of Pentacles arrives on the scene bringing news of money, prosperity, or the sensual side of a relationship. He represents the fiery part of earth, passionate and willing to commit to a relationship. Taurus rules the Knight of Pentacles, and this earthy and sensuous Knight may bring with him an invitation or a proposal of some sort. As with all Knights, he is a messenger. This messenger brings news of commitments, gifts, and offerings.

The Knight wears a red tunic for passion and a green plume for prosperity upon his helmet. He sits upon a black horse that is well fed, strong, and also adorned in the colors of passion and prosperity. The horse exudes the energy of the suit, stability. The Knight holds a pentacle in his hand, as if preparing to offer it as a gift.

As the horse and rider are facing to the right, this card can indicate forward movement, an advance in career or relationship.

In relationships, the Knight of Pentacles pursues his interest with great sensuous and passionate intensity. He offers a commitment; the Pentacle he holds forth indicates he wishes to give stability and prosperity to his intended. The appearance of the Knight of Pentacles in a spread can indicate a marriage proposal; it always indicates the offering of a commitment of some sort. In career matters, this card will indicate a job offer being presented.

In other matters, look for commitment and an offering of support of a material or emotional nature.

The negative connotation of this card implies that one may be interested in using your assets for their own personal gain.

To divine the intentions of another when this card is present you can be sure that they will offer their support concerning your situation. The energy of this card indicates that they will likely make an offering of assistance and follow through on any commitments that they make to you. Individuals under the influence of this card will be supportive of you and stick things out until the matter at hand is resolved.

In matters of timing, look to the twelfth week of Winter and for shorter-term concerns look to twelve days or twelve weeks. This card can also indicate timing occurring during the time that the Sun transits Taurus.

Contrary to popular interpretation, the Knight of Pentacles is unlikely to represent a young man with dark hair. If the physical interpretations of the Tarot were to hold true to the depictions in the artwork on the cards, all physical descriptions would be limited to members of the Caucasian race. To truly understand the card, look to the personality and energies of the card for a description of the individual; do not try to describe physical attributes. Many traditional readers do not expand their interpretations beyond the physical.

Court cards appearing in spreads do not necessarily represent people; they may well be solely representative of the energy in a situation and not a person.

The Queen of Pentacles

She enjoys being sensual and nurturing. She wants to care for and please all who approach her. She is earthy, analytical and symbolic of feminine sensuality. She is ruled by the mercurial and yet earthy nature of Virgo. She welcomes the attraction that men have for her and uses it to her advantage, making the most of her feminine wiles.

The Queen of Pentacles is the watery part of earth, she is fertile and creative. All that she commits to seems to flourish.

She sits upon her throne, adorned with fruit to symbolize her fertility, angels to indicate her level of enlightenment, the head of a goat, indicating her grounded nature and representing the astrological sign of Capricorn, also under her rule. She is amidst a bountiful garden, holding a pentacle caringly in her hands, she appears to nurture the pentacle. She is dressed in the colors of prosperity, passion and enlightenment. She brings a soft and creative energy to all she comes in contact with; well knowing that in order to succeed one must remain attentive.

She has a calm, intelligent and supportive nature. She draws men to her by her earthiness; they sense her fertility and wish to sustain it with her.

In relationship readings, this Queen will indicate a competent, though materialistic woman. She is commitment minded, but takes good care of those she holds affection for. She can indicate an upcoming commitment as well. She is a woman who revels in her sensual creativity and draws or repels people through the sense of security and comfort she emanates.

In other matters, the influence of this Queen will reflect an individual with this type of nature within the focus of the query or this energy manifesting within the Querent them self. A supportive and nurturing energy can be expected.

The negative tone of this card is the use of her feminine charms to manipulate those around her in order to get what she wants; a victim mentality may become apparent in order to satisfy her desires.

To divine the intentions of another when this card appears in a spread be aware that the person you are inquiring about will behave in a creative, supportive and nurturing way, but they may also expect a return on their investment.

In matters of timing, look to the thirteenth week of Winter for long-term concerns and the thirteenth day or week for shorter-term concerns. This card can also indicate timing occurring during the time that the Sun transits Virgo.

Contrary to popular interpretation, the Queen of Pentacles is unlikely to represent a woman with dark hair. If the physical interpretations of the Tarot were to hold true to the depictions in the artwork on the cards, all physical descriptions would be limited to members of the Caucasian race. To truly understand the card, look to the personality and energies of the card for a description of the individual; do not try to describe physical attributes. Many traditional readers do not expand their interpretations beyond the physical.

Court cards appearing in spreads do not necessarily represent people; they may well be solely representative of the energy in a situation and not a person.

The King of Pentacles

The King of Pentacles is Capricorn personified. He is the ultimate father figure. The King of Pentacles is the King of the element of earth and rules with compassion and concern for those he feels he is responsible for. He is a hard worker and an excellent provider for the material comforts of life. This King generally represents a man who is married and mature; he holds true to his commitments and expects others to do the same. This King is considered to be a prosperous man.

He represents the airy part of earth, that which can be spread on the wind to prosper and regenerate.

Again, as in all the court cards of the Suit of Pentacles, we see the King adorned in the colors of passion, prosperity and enlightenment, yellow, green and red. The King sits upon a throne adorned with bulls, representative of the element of earth, for strength and stability, and also of Taurus, one of the signs he rules. His golden crown rests upon a red hood for passion and a green wreath for creativity, fertility and prosperity. His foot rests upon the head of a lion, indicating that he has tamed his excessive passions. The top of the crown bears red flowers, again relating to his passion and creativity. He glances downward toward the Pentacle on his knee, ever mindful of the five elements it pertains to, earth, air, fire, water and spirit.

This King enjoys guiding those he cares for to make the most of their abilities and supporting their pursuits both materially and emotionally.

In relationship readings he will generally represent a man who is committed to the woman he loves, yet she may feel that his career is a rival for his attention. He has a strong need for material security even to the point where he may neglect the emotional side of his relationships. He will tend to put the needs of others before his own if forced to choose. He will sublimate his sorrows through overachievement.

This man requires that his home be a stable environment and will not allow excessive drama into his life.

When this card appears in spreads relating to other matters, you are looking at a material level of support and you will be expected to produce a return on that investment.

The negative tone of this card is a leaning toward detachment and isolation in order to avoid emotional confrontations.

To divine the intentions of others when this card appears be assured that you will gain the support of those in a position of material stability but you will be expected to produce.

Contrary to popular interpretation, the King of Pentacles is unlikely to represent a man with brunette hair. If the physical interpretations of the Tarot were to hold true to the depictions in the artwork on the cards, all physical descriptions would be limited to members of the Caucasian race. To truly understand the card, look to the personality and energies of the card for a description of the individual; do not try to describe physical attributes. Many traditional readers do not expand their interpretations beyond the physical.

Court cards appearing in spreads do not necessarily represent people; they may well be solely representative of the energy in a situation and not a person.

Reading the Cards

Uncloaking the Tarot:

Fundamentals of the Celtic Cross Spread

The Celtic Cross Spread

There are many, many varied and useful Tarot Spreads. There are also multiple variations of the Celtic Cross Spread. This is one variation of the ancient Celtic Cross Spread which is useful in providing readings for self and others.

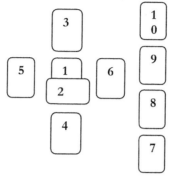

Position 1 – The Significator, the influences surrounding the Querent at this time. What is on the Querent's mind or the influences surrounding the Querent at this time.

Position 2 – The Crossing Card, forces working for or against the Querent at this time.

Position 3 – The Crowning Card, the influence that is hanging over the entire situation at this time.

Position 4 – The Base of the Matter, already a part of the Querent's experience.

Position 5 – Present and Passing, the influences that are active in the Querent's life at this time, but are exiting at the time of the reading.

Position 6 – Immediate Future, what the Querent can expect within the next two to three weeks.

Position 7 – Near Future, what the Querent can expect within the next three weeks to two months if they maintain the current path.

Position 8 – How friends and family view the situation.

Position 9 – Hopes and Fears of the Querent.

Position 10 – The Ultimate Outcome of the matter at hand if the Querent maintains the same behaviors.

The Reading

Shuffling the Cards

The key to a good Tarot Reading is the level of concentration that you and your Querent maintain. I prefer to have the Querent shuffle the cards while focusing on the matter they are concerned with, until the cards feel comfortable resting in their hands. If the Querent prefers to have a general reading rather than ask a specific question, I ask them to relax and clear their mind while shuffling. In either case, once the Querent is comfortable with the cards I ask them to cut the deck into three stacks, with their left hand, toward their left. The reason I do this is because the left hand is ruled by the right brain, which contains our subconscious thoughts, and the left hand is directly connected to the heart, where our true desires lie.

Once the Querent has cut the deck, I pick the cards up from my left to my right and lay the cards out as detailed in the diagram provided, and begin to read.

If the Querent is not physically present to handle the deck, I will shuffle and cut the cards on their behalf while we both focus on their specific question. I do not provide a general reading if the Querent cannot physically handle the cards, as the energy is just not present to promote clarity, such as when I read for a Querent over the phone.

Interpreting the Spread

As a novice at reading you may need to refer to the diagrams and interpretations while working through the positions in the spread. It is very important to try to make the reading flow from card to card and focus on what circumstances could make sometimes seemingly unrelated cards follow one another. It is very helpful to ask questions of the Querent. The Tarot is a spiritual and psychological tool and psychic abilities, so to speak, are not required to provide a comprehensive reading, but a strong sense of intuition is. Be open and honest with your Querent, assure them of the confidentiality that you will maintain, and build good communication with your subjects, this will assist the Querent in opening up to you as to what they really wish to know, and thus allow you to provide a better reading and useful insight.

Reversals and Dignities

Many Tarot Readers believe in reading reversed cards, this is not a method that proves accurate. As stated throughout the text, all of the cards of Tarot possess both a positive and a negative energy, in order to properly interpret which energy is active; you must understand the dignity of the cards on the table.

Wands, which are ruled by the element of fire, are well dignified, or to be interpreted in their primary energy when they are preceded, followed by or conjunct with the element of air, which is the element of the suit of Swords, and also when falling with another Wand. Wands are ill dignified, or to be interpreted in their secondary energy, when preceded, followed by or conjunct with the elements of water and earth, Cups and Pentacles respectively.

Cups, which are ruled by the element of water, are well dignified, or to be interpreted in their primary energy when they are preceded, followed by or conjunct with the element of earth, which is the element of the suit of Pentacles, and also when falling with another Cup. Cups are ill dignified, or to be interpreted in their secondary energy, when preceded, followed by or conjunct with the elements of fire and air, Wands and Swords respectively.

Swords, which are ruled by the element of air, are well dignified, or to be interpreted in their primary energy when they are preceded, followed by or conjunct with the element of fire, which is the element of the suit of Wands, and also when falling with another Sword. Swords are ill dignified, or to be interpreted in their secondary energy, when preceded, followed by or conjunct with the elements of water and earth, Cups and Pentacles respectively.

Pentacles, which are ruled by the element of earth, are well dignified, or to be interpreted in their primary energy when they are preceded, followed by or conjunct with the element of water, which is the element of the suit of Cups, and also when falling with another Pentacle. Pentacles are ill dignified, or to be interpreted in their secondary energy, when preceded, followed by or conjunct with the elements of fire and air, Wands and Swords respectively.

Historically, reading reversals was a short cut to learning how to understand the dignities of the cards cast, however, it has been found by this cartomancers to be a highly inaccurate method. In order to ensure that reversed cards were meant to be interpreted as such, one would have to take great care to always keep all seventy-eight cards of the deck facing the same way whenever handled. This is neither practical nor logical.

In this text, all primary interpretations are given first and the secondary energy of the card is listed second. If a card is well dignified, use the primary energy as your interpretation, if ill dignified, go to the secondary. This means that a card with a negative energy, such as the Three of Swords, will vibrate to its' more positive energy if it is followed by a Cup, making it ill dignified.

Ethics

It is my sincere hope that those who employ this book as a learning tool will adopt a code of ethics that is inclusive of referring your subjects to mainstream sources of assistance for any long term or recurring problems. Most especially concerns with health, (both physical and mental), finances, legalities, or any other life situations that may require the assistance of a trained specialist. Remember, the Tarot is a guide to enhance life, not a tool that directs the course of life, free will is always available to change our futures.